T0209177

"There is no higher value in life than experiencing the love of God, for everything else flows from that. Nancy not only explains the way, but she also paints a picture of the path for us to follow. I highly recommend this book."

—DR. JOHN TOWNSEND, PSYCHOLOGIST, RADIO HOST, AND COAUTHOR OF *Boundaries*

"This is a cozy book you will want to have at your bedside. Imagine how wonderful the day would be if you woke to some whispered reminder of how dear you were to the heart of God. Imagine how peaceful the night would be if you went to sleep with a kiss of that reminder on your forehead. These are the tender mercies this soft-spoken book has to offer."

—KEN GIRE, AUTHOR OF *Moments with the Savior, Windows of the Soul,* AND *The Divine Embrace*

"The Bible tells us 'God is love,' yet very few people act like they understand it or live like they believe it. *The Wonder of His Love* is an amazing book that will help you discover God's awesome love and radically change the way you live. If you think God is not on your side or is not doing everything He can to show you His love—read this book."

—STEPHEN ARTERBURN, FOUNDER OF NEW LIFE MINISTRIES AND COAUTHOR OF *Every Man's Battle*

"*The Wonder of His Love* is like a warm embrace from God Himself."

—BETH MOORE

THE

WONDER

of HIS LOVE

NANCY STAFFORD

MULTNOMAH
BOOKS

THE WONDER OF HIS LOVE

Published in association with the literary agency of Alive Communications, Inc.,
7680 Goddard Street, Suite 200, Colorado Springs, CO 80920
© 2004 by Nest, Inc.
International Standard Book Number: 978-1-60142-431-0

All italics in Scripture are the author's emphasis.
Unless otherwise indicated, Scripture quotations are from:
The Holy Bible, New International Version © 1973, 1984 by International Bible Society,
used by permission of Zondervan Publishing House
Other Scripture quotations are from:
The Holy Bible, King James Version (KJV)
The Living Bible (TLB) © 1971. Used by permission of Tyndale House Publishers, Inc.
All rights reserved.
Holy Bible, New Living Translation (NLT) © 1996.
Used by permission of Tyndale House Publishers, Inc. All rights reserved.
The Message © 1993, 1994, 1995, 1996, 2000, 2001, 2002
Used by permission of NavPress Publishing Group
The New Jerusalem Bible (NJB) © 1985 by Darton, Longman & Todd, Ltd.
and Doubleday & Company, Inc.
Revised Standard Version Bible (RSV) © 1946, 1952 by the Division of Christian Education
of the National Council of the Churches of Christ in the United States of America
The New Testament in Modern English, Revised Edition (Phillips)
© 1958, 1960, 1972 by J. B. Phillips
The Holy Bible, English Standard Version (ESV) © 2001 by Crossway Bibles,
a division of Good News Publishers. Used by permission. All rights reserved.

Published in the United States by Multnomah, an imprint of Random House,
a division of Penguin Random House LLC, New York.

MULTNOMAH® and its mountain colophon are registered trademarks
of Penguin Random House LLC.

The Library of Congress has cataloged the original edition as follows:

Stafford, Nancy.
 The wonder of His love / by Nancy Stafford.
    p. cm.
  ISBN 1-59052-325-3 (pbk.)
  1. God—Love. I. Title.
  BT140.S7193 2004
  231'.6—dc22

                              2004007348

This book is for anyone who is starved for wonder, who yearns to venture deeper into the heart—and arms—of the Father, who longs to glimpse the wonder of His love.

Thank You...

Heartfelt thanks to my friend and champion at Multnomah, Bill Jensen, for your continuous support and affirmation and for entrusting me with this wondrous message of God's love. My gratitude to my editors, Judith St. Pierre, for your friendship, skill, and sensitivity, and Larry Libby, for your insightful contributions, kindness, and great encouragement. Thank you, Jennifer Gott, for "being there" and for all your gracious help. Many thanks to my precious mother and my brother Tracy, my friends and steadfast "prayer gals," especially Gayle Miller and Mylin Stoddard. To my husband, Larry, thank you for demonstrating God's faithful and gentle love to me every single day of my life. And with my whole heart I thank my Lord—whose love leaves me in perpetual wonder and takes my breath away.

Contents

STARVED FOR *Wonder*

I will praise you, O LORD, with all my heart;
I will tell of all your wonders.

PSALM 9:1

*T*HE WORLD WILL NEVER starve for wonders," G. K. Chesterton wrote, "but only for want of wonder." I have written this book because I am starved for wonder. I yearn to shake off the mundane and crack open my jaded heart so God can fill it with the vastness and reality and wonder of His love.

I need to grasp the wonder of God's love because my own love is found wanting. I do not love as God loves. I fall so short. Too often my heart is slammed shut, crusty tight.

Even when I feel love there, I don't always express it, don't follow through with actions that embody true love—forgiveness, long-suffering, sacrifice—the very acts of love that God has demonstrated for millennia.

Psalm 9:1 says: "I will tell of all your wonders." In Hebrew, *tell of* actually means *declare.* Praise is not just a private meditation on the wonders of the Lord, but a public declaration of them. This book is a humble attempt at a twenty-first-century version of Psalm 9:1—a public declaration and celebration of God's glorious virtues, righteous deeds, and the wonder of His love for us.

What difference would it make in your life if you spent the next month or so thinking about the love of God? In some ways, it would be like walking along the edge of a vast ocean, for it would take volumes and volumes to exhaust the subject of His great love for us—so many that, as John said, "even the whole world would not have room for the books that would be written" (John 21:25).

Yet *The Wonder of His Love* invites you to wade into that endless sea. Through reflections on God's love, from the wonder of Creation to the wonder of the Cross, I invite you to feel the caress of the gentle surf, and then journey deeper still and experience the thunder of the breakers. I pray, as Paul prayed for the church at Ephesus, that you will grasp how "wide and long and high and deep is the love of Christ" (3:18). I pray that you will sense God's whispered invitation to "taste and see" (Psalm 34:8) that He is a good, trustworthy, matchless lover, "compassionate and gracious…abounding in love and faithfulness" (86:15).

I so desperately need to be reminded of God's love for me. I bet you do, too.

So come with me into the mystery and majesty of God's unfathomable love. Let's shake off the lethargy, soften our jaded attitudes, and crack open our hearts. Let's journey together into the heart of God. Let's let the wonder come....

We're starved for it.

INITIATING
*L*OVE

We love because he first loved us.

1 JOHN 4:19

*L*OVE COULD NOT BE contained. Love compelled Him. Love had to create life.

So He hurled countless galaxies into space and saturated the heavens with planets and stars. Then Love burst forth on the earth. He stored up symphonies in the throats of songbirds, splashed masterpieces across mountains, slipped secret paintings inside shells.

All that He spoke into being, all that Love created, was for you.

You were His motivation. When God created the heavens and the earth, He thought of you...and then worked backwards. He sprinkled stars in the sky so that you could lie on a quilt on summer evenings and watch them flicker. He blew gardenia-scented breezes to kiss your face and unleashed thundering waterfalls to awaken your soul. He formed hidden reefs, secret worlds of unimagined beauty, and tucked them away in the oceans for you to explore.

He filled the earth with beauty to make His love visible. "In order that we finite beings may apprehend the Emperor," Charles Williams wrote, "He translates His glory into multiple forms—into stars, woods, waters, beasts, and the bodies of men."[1] Man was not just the final item on a divine to-do list. Man is the pièce de résistance, the coup de grâce, the grand finale.

Before God imagined the galaxies or invented history, He dreamed of us. Infinite Love thought first of companionship; He created us for relationship with Him. After He hung the stars and the moon, spread the fields with flowers, draped the forests with green canopies, and filled the air with fragrance and music, He prepared a special place where He could have fellowship with His greatest creation.

A garden was our first home. Eden was an earthly paradise, perfect and bountiful, a brilliant reflection of the nature and love of God. In this Garden, in this shimmering, misty jewel, He wrote the message of His love, and when everything was ready, He created us from dust and bone.

For a time, all was well in Paradise. Our parents, Adam and Eve, walked with Him and talked with Him. There was intimacy between created and Creator. They were His own. Then sin entered the Garden, and with it came the Fall in every individual life. Our sin severed the relationship with Him for which we were created.

But God loved us so much that He was not willing to let us go. He still wanted fellowship with us. He still yearned for companionship and intimacy with us. Love could not give up on His beloved. "For the sake of his great name the LORD will not reject his people, because the LORD was pleased to make you his own" (1 Samuel 12:22).

God had a plan to redeem His creation, so in His love He sent His Son to earth. God expressed His love to us in a garden, first in Eden…and then in another garden, Gethsemane, to show that He was still Emmanuel, *God with us*. Christ, the new Adam, came to undo the damage of Eden. "It cost God nothing, so far as we know, to create nice things," C. S. Lewis wrote, "but to convert rebellious wills cost Him crucifixion."[2]

What kind of God is this who would not give up on such wayward, sinful people? What kind of God would send His only Son to die so we could live with Him forever? What kind of God would create galaxies, angels, and natural wonders…and yet stoop to love us?

"To whom will you compare me?
Or who is my equal?" says the Holy One.
Lift your eyes and look to the heavens:
Who created all these?
He who brings out the starry host one by one,
and calls them each by name.
Because of his great power and mighty strength,
not one of them is missing.
Do you not know?
Have you not heard?
The LORD is the everlasting God,
the Creator of the ends of the earth.
He will not grow tired or weary,
and his understanding no one can fathom.

ISAIAH 40:25–26, 28

Our God is all-knowing and all-powerful, and everything He does comes from His inexhaustible love. "Your love, O LORD, reaches to the heavens, your faithfulness to the skies" (Psalm 36:5). The One who created the cosmos created me. The One who knows everything about the universe knows everything about me. The One who sustains all things sustains me.

- He sets planets in space...and plants dreams deep within my soul.
- He spreads deserts with sand...and sprinkles me with His cleansing blood.
- He decrees rulers and thrones...and proclaims my heart His resting place.
- He erases nations from the earth...and wipes every tear from my eye.
- He thunders in the tempest...and whispers love songs to my heart.
- He covers my sin...and unveils Himself to me.

In mountains and woods and rocks, I see God's footprint. In ocean waves and whispered winds, I hear His voice. In gusts through pines and warm desert breezes, I feel His hand on my cheek. And in a fiery sunset, I glimpse the glory of His robe.

This God of creation, the Sovereign of the universe, wants to be with us. Though we have rebelled against Him, He offers to redeem us. Though we have distanced ourselves, He invites us into fellowship. Love initiated all creation, and Love initiated our redemption. And in eternity to come, as we walk together through wondrous new creations, we will stand in perpetual awe of the wonder of His love.

Lord, I marvel that Your love is so great

that even heaven could not contain it.

It burst forth everywhere—in nature,

mankind…and my heart.

You have become the unutterable sigh

in the depth of my soul.

Your love initiated everything.

I could not seek You unless You first sought me.

I love You only because You first loved me.

Yet try as I may, my capacity to love You

is but a millionth degree of

Your unfathomable love for me.

Help me to grasp the wonder of Your great love!

Amen

RESURRECTING

OVE

"I am the resurrection and the life.
He who believes in me will live, even though he dies;
and whoever lives and believes in me will never die.
Do you believe this?"

JOHN 11:25–26

MANY HAVE SPECULATED
that the site of Jesus' burial and resurrection lies somewhere
within the Church of the Holy Sepulcher, inside the walls of
the Old City of Jerusalem. But I believe it was the Garden
Tomb, just outside the walls.

Several years ago I walked through that tranquil garden,

lush with greenery and wildlife, and then stooped and entered the tomb. A soft beam of light spilled into the darkened room, revealing the place where His body would have been laid.

As I stood alone in that still place, reflecting on Jesus' resurrection, I imagined what it would have been like to be there with Mary Magdalene and Mary the wife of Clopas when they saw that shining angel and heard him tell them not to be afraid, but to come see the place where Jesus had lain. I could almost hear an otherworldly murmur, a sound like an angel's sigh, "He is not here; he has risen, just as he said" (Matthew 28:6).

It's hard to comprehend the wonder of Jesus' resurrection, harder still to grasp the miracle that because He rose again, we too are resurrected. He knows how cynical and fearful we can be, how full of doubt and empty of faith. But Love asks us to receive this new life…through belief.

Mark tells the story of Jairus, a synagogue ruler whose twelve-year-old daughter was at the point of death (Mark 5:21–42). Heartsick and gripped with fear, he begged Jesus to come to her. Jesus was following Jarius home when messengers arrived with the news that the girl had died.

"Your daughter's *dead* already," they said. "Don't bother the teacher!" But Jairus—and Jesus—ignored them. "Don't be afraid," Jesus said. "Just believe." He took the child by the hand and said, "Little girl, I say to you, get up!" And immediately she rose and walked around.

Luke tells of the resurrection of the only son of a widow

from Nain. After Jesus raised the son from the dead, the people "were all filled with awe and praised God. 'A great prophet has appeared among us,' they said. 'God has come to help his people'" (Luke 7:16).

And so He has. But how slow we are to believe it!

John tells us about the resurrection of Lazarus. Four days after he died, his sisters heard that Jesus was coming. Martha went out to meet him, and they had a rather strange conversation:

> Martha said to Jesus, "Lord, if you had been here, my brother would not have died. But even now I know that whatever you ask from God, God will give you." Jesus said to her, "Your brother will rise again." Martha said to him, "I know that he will rise again in the resurrection on the last day." Jesus said to her, "I am the resurrection and the life. Whoever believes in me, though he die, yet shall he live, and everyone who lives and believes in me shall never die. Do you believe this?" She said to him, "Yes, Lord; I believe that you are the Christ, the Son of God, who is coming into the world."
>
> JOHN 11:21-27, ESV

Martha was certain that Jesus was the Son of God, the long-awaited Messiah, and she was even convinced that Jesus could raise Lazarus. But she didn't really believe it was going to happen. When Jesus ordered the stone rolled away, she protested. Lazarus was too far gone.

When Martha and Jesus finished speaking, Martha went to tell Mary that Jesus wanted to see her. With her grieving friends following her, Mary went to Jesus and fell at His feet. Then she said exactly the same thing Martha had said: "Master, if only you had been here, my brother would not have died" (v. 32, *The Message*).

John says:

> When Jesus saw her sobbing and the Jews with her sobbing, a deep anger welled up within him.
> He said, "Where did you put him?"
> "Master, come and see," they said.
> Now Jesus wept.
>
> VV. 33–35, *THE MESSAGE*

I don't believe Jesus was weeping for Lazarus. After all, He knew what He was about to do. I think He was weeping because of unbelief. He was trying to tell them that He *is* the resurrection—not just in *that* day, but right now, today, this moment. And they just didn't get it. I can only imagine that because of our unbelief, Jesus weeps for us, too.

There's another resurrection story, but you won't find it in the pages of Scripture. It's mine.

When Jesus rose from the dead, the first person He appeared to was Mary Magdalene, a woman from whom He had driven seven demons. I love it that the one who had had so little hope, the one who was most consumed by darkness, was the one who saw Him first. I like to think that if I had been there that day, perhaps He would have revealed Himself to me first.

Before Christ gave me new life, I was a lot like Mary. Stone-cold dead in a tomb of my own making. Wearing the grave clothes of selfishness, brokenness, and sin. Searching for love in romantic entanglements. Desperately looking for life in religions and philosophies.

You would think I was too far gone.

But Jesus didn't. He rolled away the stone that was my heart, took my hand, and shouted, "My daughter—get up!"

Someday, after we have shed our failing, mortal bodies, those who believe in Him will be outfitted in glorious new bodies, made to live eternally with Him. But we don't have to wait for that day to enjoy the wonder of our resurrection. "I tell you the truth, whoever hears my word and believes him who sent me *has* eternal life and will not be condemned; he *has crossed* over from death to life" (John 5:24).

Present tense. Here and now. Love asks only that we believe.

Lord, I am in awe when

I think of Your resurrection

and am overwhelmed that because

You live, so do I!

You have brought me from death to life.

Help me to receive, through faith,

all that my new life in You really means.

Thank You that the eternal life You

give is not just for the future, but includes today.

Help me to live each day full of life,

full of hope, full of faith!

Amen

ACCESSIBLE

OVE

*Let us therefore come boldly
unto the throne of grace,
that we may obtain mercy,
and find grace to help in time of need.*

HEBREWS 4:16, KJV

*I*N THE BOOK OF REVELATION,
the apostle John describes a mind-boggling scene. Blinding
light, bouncing and refracting off otherworldly colors—
jasper and emerald and carnelian. A multifaceted rainbow
encircling a throne, with throne upon throne surrounding it.
Blazing lamp stands, living creatures, flashes of lightning,
peals of thunder.

It is terrifying.

It is beautiful.

It is the throne of the living God.

And Jesus invites John to come close. "Come," the Lord says to him. "Come up here."

Centuries earlier, the Israelites had watched God descend on Mount Sinai in a thick cloud of fire and smoke accompanied by lightning and thunder and blasting trumpet sounds. Louder and louder grew the deafening trumpet blasts, while smoke billowed as if from a raging furnace. God's supernatural sound-and-light show made the entire mountain—and all the people—tremble violently.

On that day, Moses and the Israelites got a glimpse of what is going on in heaven continually. Perhaps God's holiness is so great, so inexpressible, so incalculable, that it cannot be contained, even in heaven, so His glory and righteousness and justice simply erupt into the atmosphere by their sheer power and magnitude.

The throne of God. A place of unfathomable beauty and holy terror.

Who dares approach?

The Israelites were forbidden to go up the mountain— or even so much as touch the base of it—on penalty of death. Only Moses was permitted to ascend that holy hill, and even he was not permitted to see God face-to-face, lest he die as well.

Yet God invited John to come. And He invites you and me. What a wonder!

God forbade the Israelites to come, warned them most sternly *not* to come, yet He invites us to come close. God's invitation is based not on our merit, but on what His Son did on the cross. Through His death, Jesus became the High Priest of a New Covenant, the sacrifice needed to grant us access to the Father. Jesus entered the Most Holy Place once for all by His own blood (Hebrews 9:12). The veil separating heaven and earth was torn asunder, the door to heaven swung wide, and now God invites us to come.

Because of Jesus, we all have access to that mighty throne. Even so, many of us are afraid to be in His presence. We're so afraid that if God knew us, *really* knew us, He would thunder and rail and throw lightning spears at us. Or at least turn away in disgust. *He wouldn't accept me,* we think. *He wouldn't receive me. He couldn't possibly embrace me.*

So we do everything we can to earn the right to enter the throne room. We strive to keep the Ten Commandments and follow the Golden Rule—after all, that's in the Bible somewhere, isn't it? We try to be good and moral, impose can'ts and shouldn'ts, and work at being religious—go to church, tithe, follow certain rituals, repeat certain prayers.

That should work.

But God says no. "My Son has taken care of all that. I want *you*. Come...."

This same God who shrouds Himself in lightning-charged smoke, whose voice sounds like trumpet blasts and thunder cracks, this holy God, enthroned on a crystal sea and enveloped by angelic praise, invites us to approach Him, beckons us to come close. It can't be. It shouldn't be. But somehow, it is. Hebrews 4:16 urges us to "approach the throne of grace with confidence, so that we may receive mercy and find grace to help us in our time of need."

Whenever I reflect on that amazing verse, I think of that now famous photograph of President Kennedy working at his desk in the Oval Office, signing bills, peace treaties, and history-making executive orders. And at his feet, playing on the carpet under his desk, is his young son, John Jr.

I've always imagined countless cabinet members, senators, and dignitaries lined up outside that office door, waiting for access to that inner sanctum, waiting to be invited in, each hoping to find favor. And there at the feet of the world's most powerful man is his son, a toddler, playing with his toys. Confident in his father's love and affection, the little boy is completely carefree, happy, and at home in the presence of his daddy.

That scene strikes me as the perfect picture of the access we all have to the One who sits on the heavenly throne. Read this verse and see if your heart doesn't soar!

Therefore, brothers, since we have confidence to enter the Most Holy Place by the blood of Jesus, by a new and living way opened for us through the curtain, that is, his body, and since we have a great priest over the house of God, let us draw near to God with a sincere heart in full assurance of faith, having our hearts sprinkled to cleanse us from a guilty conscience and having our bodies washed with pure water. Let us hold unswervingly to the hope we profess, for he who promised is faithful.

HEBREWS 10:19–23

We are His children, and whenever we need His grace and mercy, His tender lovingkindness, He bids us come. He invites us to enter His throne room. You have unhindered, unhurried personal access to a living God who loves you, desires you, and has wonderful intentions for you. Take your loving Father at His word and come boldly to the throne of grace!

He's inviting you in.

Father, thank You that I can come

to You whenever I wish.

Your arms are open wide—

because of Jesus, I have complete access to You.

Forgive me for the times I forget that.

I choose to come boldly into Your presence—

today and every day.

Help me to overcome anything that hinders,

anything that would keep me from intimacy with You.

Thank You that this wondrous invitation

is my divine birthright as Your child.

Amen

COVERING
Love

You forgave the iniquity of your people
and covered all their sins.

Psalm 85:2

O NE EVENING AS I REACHED
for the check after dinner, my friend grabbed it, shook her
head, and smiled.

"It's covered!" she said.

I appreciated her generous act. I really did. But I have to
admit I had a tough time accepting it. For some reason it's
difficult for me to let somebody else pay the tab. As I
watched my friend pay for my dinner, it struck me that

many of us experience the same difficulty in our relationship with God. We have trouble accepting that "it's covered."

I thought of another friend, Ann, who has had a hard time receiving the love and forgiveness of God. Although she has a growing relationship with Him, she has often felt that He couldn't *possibly* forgive her for all she has done. She has made some mammoth mistakes in her life: got pregnant as a teenager, had an abortion, got married and divorced twice, did drugs.

Then the day came when Ann confessed her sins to God and He covered them. Completely. Yet even though she *knew* she was forgiven, she didn't always *feel* forgiven. She had a hard time letting go of her past. Sometimes when the memories closed in on her, she was plagued with guilt and shame and had a hard time sleeping at night.

Then came a turning point that helped her understand this loving God who completely covers our sins. One sleepless night she sensed that Jesus was close to her. She had always loved the psalmist's assurance that "He will cover you with his feathers, and under his wings you will find refuge" (Psalm 91:4). And that night she had a mental picture of herself pulling up just the tiniest edge of the very corner of His robe to cover herself. Feeling protected, she fell asleep. Then sometime during the night she sensed Jesus' overwhelming love for her, and she realized that He had covered her completely as she slept. It was just as the prophet Isaiah promised our Messiah would do: "He has clothed me with the garments of salvation, he has covered me with the robe of righteousness" (Isaiah 61:10, RSV).

Ann finally understood that no matter what she had done, no matter how undeserving she felt, Jesus was covering her sin with His righteousness. She realized that when God looks at her, He sees her wearing the robes of His own Son. He sees her as cleansed, pure, and blameless. Then Ann sensed Jesus gently asking her, *Will you finally believe that "it's covered"? Will you finally receive this gift of love I've given you?*

Here is the wonder of His love: What we willingly expose, God graciously covers; what we refuse to cover up, He covers for us. "If we confess our sins," says the apostle John, "he is faithful and just and will forgive us our sins and purify us from all unrighteousness" (1 John 1:9). When we expose our sin, God forgives it—all because of what Jesus did on the cross.

God is a righteous judge, full of justice and truth, and He says, "Without the shedding of blood there is no forgiveness" (Hebrews 9:22). To satisfy His demand for justice, blood had to be shed to pay the penalty for our sin. In the Old Testament that sacrifice was a lamb, perfect and unblemished. But it wasn't enough. The worshipers were never cleansed once and for all; the sacrifice had to be repeated year after year. The lamb simply foreshadowed the one perfect sacrifice.

Then God sent His Son. Jesus clothed Himself in humanity and came to earth for the express purpose of dying. He was the perfect, unblemished Lamb of God. Though He Himself was without sin, He took the blame for all our sins and paid our debt—*in full.* Peter says that "love covers over a multitude of sins" (1 Peter 4:8). In a miracle of love, Christ died to cover the sins of everyone who accepts the gift of God's forgiveness. Jesus' words from the cross—"It is finished"—are a triumphant shout of "It is covered!" Jesus has already covered *all* our mistakes, *all* our failings, *all* our shortcomings. And as we keep exposing new areas of weakness and sin in our lives, as we keep uncovering our failings and wrongdoings, He keeps covering them for us.

This love flies in the face of everything we know. In a world intent on cover-ups and good impressions, He invites raw exposure. And then when we repent, He covers our shame with His goodness and our disgrace with His holiness.

How about you? Do you have a hard time believing that God loves you and has completely forgiven you? That your past and your sins have been covered and you don't have to pay for what you've done? Do you keep reaching for the tab? If so, Christ wants to show you what He showed Ann: "It's covered!" King David, who made some mammoth mistakes himself, wrote: "I acknowledged my sin to you and did not cover up my iniquity.... Blessed is he whose transgressions are forgiven, whose sins are covered" (Psalm 32:5, 1).

The King of the universe, who blankets the night skies with black velvet and glimmering stars, who drapes the mountains with snowdrifts and covers the deep with oceans, comes to each of us and uncovers our heart, unveils our fears, and then covers us up again with Himself. So let's rip off the veil, strip off the mask. Give Him the truth. Give Him your weakness. Give Him your sin.

And as you do…His love will cover you. What a wonder.

Father, forgive me for the times when,

in pride or unbelief,

I feel that I have to pay my own debt.

Once and for all I receive the

gift of complete forgiveness

I possess through Christ.

When I am tempted to live in shame,

hang on to the past, or doubt Your forgiveness,

remind me of the Cross.

When I am tempted to conceal

my sin or hide my weakness,

remind me of Your continuing, covering love.

Amen

DREAMING

OVE

> *"Enlarge the place of your tent,*
> *stretch your tent curtains wide,*
> *do not hold back; lengthen your cords,*
> *strengthen your stakes."*
>
> ISAIAH 54:2

AH, PETER...IMPULSIVE, impetuous Peter.

I think of him that day on the mountaintop, when he and James and John watched in awe as Jesus, His face shining like the sun and His clothes as bright as light, spoke face-to-face with Moses and Elijah. An experience of such wonder, such terrible majesty, would leave most of us speech-less.

But not Peter. Peter was rarely at a loss for words.

"Rabbi," he babbled, "it is good that we are here. Let us make three tents, one for you and one for Moses and one for Elijah" (Mark 9:5, ESV). In the early days of his discipleship, Peter almost always said the first thing that came to his mind—and he usually got it all wrong.

What was running through Peter's mind? It could have been a prophecy from the book of Amos: "In that day I will restore David's fallen tent" (9:11). This was Peter's dream. And he wanted to do whatever he could to help make it come true—even if it meant building tents so Jesus and Elijah and Moses would stay there on the mountain. Jesus had already told him that He had to suffer and go away first, but Peter hadn't been listening. He wanted the kingdom to begin now—on *this* day, not *that* day. He wanted the glory without the suffering. He wanted the crown without the cross. Fixed on his own dream, Peter forgot that God had called him to be a fisher of men. Not a tentmaker.

Have you ever wondered why Peter, with all his faults, was one of Jesus' closest disciples? I think it was because he dreamed big for God and went for it. His problem wasn't lack of zeal; *his problem was his tendency not to listen enough and to lose his focus.* To know that your dream is from God, you have to listen to Him. And then when you hear Him and step out in faith, you have to keep your eyes on Him, not on what's going on around you.

I know of just two people who have ever walked on water. Why was Peter one of them? Because he knew for certain that Jesus was the one calling him out.

"Lord, if it's you," he said, "bid me come."

"Come," Jesus said.

And then Peter did something he had never before dreamed of doing—he walked on water. And as long as he kept his eyes on Jesus, he kept on walking. It was only when he lost his focus that he began to sink.

Most of us dream too small. Dare to get out of the boat! Sure, when you're out on the water, you're going to get wet. But at least you'll be out there. You'll be closer to Jesus than the ones back in the boat, and He will reach out His hand to catch you if you start to sink.

God is a big God. Invite Him into your dreams and ask Him to show you His dreams for you. Then listen to Him…and His dreams will become yours. Refuse to settle for less than His perfect will, His path of destiny for you. Don't live in a rut, clinging to what's safe and familiar. You already know how much He loves you. Let Him show you the great plans He has for you, the specific things He's put in your heart that only *you* can fulfill. And if you've once dreamed, but your dream has died, let the experience of Peter encourage you.

After vowing that he would *never* deny Jesus, Peter proceeded to deny Him three times. Then Christ was crucified, and Peter's dream died with Him. He went back to fishing. Back to the old boat and back to the old rut. And he wasn't alone. Six other disciples, including James and John, were right there with him. They worked all night at their old profession—and caught nothing at all.

Then a stranger appeared on the shore and asked if they'd caught anything. When they said no, he told them that they were fishing on the wrong side of the boat. Try the right side, he said. They listened, followed his advice…and caught so many fish that they couldn't haul them all in. John was first to recognize the stranger. "It is the Lord!" he cried (John 21:7).

When Peter heard that, he again climbed out of the boat. But this time he didn't walk. He jumped into the water, swam to shore, and waded into the Lord's presence. Standing there dripping wet, feeling like an utter failure, he found himself face-to-face with the resurrected Savior he had denied.

Jesus, however, didn't accuse him or reprimand him. He simply asked a question. "Peter do you love me?" He asked him that question three times—once for each time Peter had denied Him. And each time in response, Peter said yes. "Then feed my lambs," Jesus said.

All along, this had been God's dream for Peter, the destiny He had called him to back on the shores of Galilee when they first met. And now, in the soft, slanted light of sunrise, He took him back to the dream. On the day of Pentecost, it was Peter who explained to the gathered crowd that the tongues they heard were the outpouring of the Holy Spirit. Peter was back in the realm of visions and dreams, fishing for men and inviting God's lost sheep back into the fold. Peter's failures did not change God's dream for him, and your failures haven't changed His dreams for you.

Dream big for God! Enlarge your tents, stretch your tent curtains wide, and don't hold back. Just don't waste time trying to build tents if God has called you to fish for men and feed sheep. Let Him show you His dream for you—and then follow it to the ends of the earth. It's far greater than anything you could dream for yourself. And know that if God has called you to do something, He will carry it to completion. The outcome is up to Him.

Our part is to listen to Him and keep our eyes on Him…and then get out of the boat.

Lord, show me Your dream for my life.

Exchange my desires for Yours.

Remove fear and doubt and disbelief.

Breathe life into my dashed dreams,

and renew my hope.

Help me to listen to You,

keep my eyes on You, and follow You.

Use me, Lord, in ways that are more wonderful

than I ever could have dreamed or imagined!

Amen

EMPOWERING

LOVE

I can do all things through
Christ who strengthens me.
PHILIPPIANS 4:13, NKJV

HAVE A BEAUTIFUL FRIEND,
Mary, who is just beginning to experience what genuine love
is all about. Mary told me that the night before she married
Bob, she couldn't sleep a wink. It wasn't the excitement that
caused her insomnia; it was sheer panic. At 2 A.M. her heart
was racing. She broke into a sweat and had to take a shower
to cool off and calm down.

Hours away from her second wedding, with tears

streaming down her face, Mary stood in the shower remembering what the minister had read at her first wedding. She didn't know much of the Bible by heart, but she did know this passage from the apostle Paul's letter to the Corinthians, and she repeated the verses over and over through her tears:

> Love is patient, love is kind. It does not envy, it does not boast, it is not proud. It is not rude, it is not self-seeking, it is not easily angered, it keeps no record of wrongs. Love does not delight in evil but rejoices with the truth. It always protects, always trusts, always hopes, always perseveres. Love never fails.
>
> 1 CORINTHIANS 13:4–8

It's impossible! Mary wept. *I can never do these things. I don't have it in me! I'm going to blow this—again!* She was terrified.

The next day she and Bob went downtown alone—they wouldn't let anyone go with them—and were married by a judge in his empty chambers. She wore a short black dress since a long white one hadn't worked out for her before. She had no flowers, nothing beautiful or sentimental to mark the day. They didn't take any photos because she didn't want another picture of failure in her life.

Today I'm happy to report that Mary and Bob have been happily married for seven years. They have a growing relationship with each other...and with God. It's been a revelation to Mary that Jesus accepts her and cherishes her unconditionally. Yet because no one had ever really given her unconditional love, she has had a hard time believing that God could really love her "no matter what."

So when she loses her patience with her husband or yells at the kids, she feels as if she has totally blown it in God's eyes. When she envies the lady down the block who has a newer car, smaller dress size, or a husband who helps more around the house, she's sure she falls so short of what God wants her to be that she slips into secret self-loathing.

She keeps trying and trying to love in the way Paul describes in 1 Corinthians 13, but she doesn't truly believe that she can ever be good *enough* or love *enough*. Her heart and mind have been programmed to think that if she falls short in any way, if she doesn't respond perfectly in every situation, if she just plain messes up—as we *all* do every day—God will walk away from her, just like all the others who abandoned her.

Recently Mary told me that she read 1 Corinthians 13 again, but this time with brand-new eyes. This time it didn't seem as if Paul was simply recording a list of qualities she should strive to achieve; he seemed to be describing a Person who had already achieved them. And as she read the familiar verses, she slowly began to recognize Jesus in the words:

Jesus is patient, Jesus is kind. Jesus does not envy, Jesus does not boast, Jesus is not proud. Jesus is not rude, Jesus is not self-seeking, Jesus is not easily angered, Jesus keeps no record of wrongs. Jesus does not delight in evil but rejoices in the truth. Jesus always protects, Jesus always trusts, Jesus always hopes, Jesus always perseveres. Jesus never fails.

All of a sudden, *love* took on a whole new meaning. Suddenly, Mary saw Paul's list not as an impossible standard of who she had to be in her own power and strength, but as the person she could be because Christ lived within her. Jesus *in* her could love others *through* her.

When Mary inserted Jesus' name in the place of *love,* her life changed, for she realized that in order to love as we're called to love, she had to rely completely on Him.

So do you and I. We can't do it on our own…and He doesn't expect us to.

The more we open ourselves to His love, the more we yield ourselves to Him, respond to His Spirit, and just let Him live His love through us, the more we show the kind of love Paul described. We could *never* love like this on our own; we could *never* love our spouse, our kids, our friends, strangers—and certainly not our enemies—that way. But the great mystery of love is this: We don't have to. "For I can do everything with the help of Christ who gives me the strength I need" (Philippians 4:13, NLT). God Himself is committed to doing it through us.

So when you're struggling, when you're envious and discontented, your marriage is stressed, your kids are rebellious, or your employer is just plain impossible, remember: *He* is the One who gives you the power to love.

Lord, I am overwhelmed at the wonder that when

You came to live in me,

You brought Your love to live in me.

You enable me to do—and to be—

more than I ever could on my own.

So live Your life through me,

extend Your grace through me,

heal and bless through me,

serve and encourage through me,

and love others extravagantly through me.

I can do all these things—because Your love

continually empowers me!

Amen

FAITHFUL

LOVE

"My faithful love will be with him....
He will call out to me, 'You are my Father,
my God, the Rock my Savior.'"

PSALM 89:24, 26

ONCE WHEN I WAS TWELVE, I went to spend the night at my girlfriend's house. She was a new friend from another state. Her parents were younger than mine, pretty and handsome, and I was amazed because they would have big parties and go out dancing. My girl-friend was pretty like her mom, dark-haired and exotic looking. She was popular and outgoing, not shy like I was. I liked being with her, and I was flabbergasted that she wanted me as her friend.

At dusk my friend made a phone call, and then we headed outside to hang out. I looked over my shoulder as we went out the door. I couldn't believe how cool her parents were—no permission needed, no checking up, no sign of them at all. Pretty soon a neighbor boy joined us with his cousin from Jacksonville, and we all stood around in the middle of the street. I was never allowed in the middle of the street in my neighborhood. (Not that I'd ever tried it; I just knew Mom would never have allowed it.)

The mosquitoes started biting, then the no-see-ums. The night-blooming jasmine was intoxicating, and the crickets were making a racket. It was a perfect south Florida evening.

Then I saw it: the orange glow of a cigarette. The neighbor boy sidled up to my friend, and she laughed a breathy, girly giggle. I'd never heard her laugh like that before. In the twilight they whispered, jostled, and teased. It looked like the mating rituals of baboons I had seen on *National Geographic* TV specials.

He offered her his cigarette. They giggled and swayed. She looked up at him coyly…then took it. When she handed it back, he slipped his arm around her shoulder, and they walked down the street and into the shadows, just as the streetlights sputtered on. She wedged herself into the crook of a mango tree, and they started kissing. Making out, really.

I panicked. *What's happening? How did I get here? I hate*

this! Sick feelings hit me like waves. That night, something changed forever. I knew then and there that growing up meant that innocence could be as fleeting as the gauzy sunset on a perfect south Florida evening. And it terrified me.

Suddenly all my adolescent protests of "You're not being *fair!* I *am* grown up! You'll *never* understand!" came crashing down. Now, after all my yearning and clamoring to be treated like a grown-up, all I wanted to do was scramble into the safety of my parents' Oldsmobile, get a Dilly Bar from the Dairy Queen, gather my dog, Daffodil, onto my lap, and sit with my mom and dad on the sofa watching TV.

I wanted to stay a little girl.

I can't even remember what I said to the cousin from Jacksonville, but I walked quickly from the street, slipped quietly into the house, and called my parents to come and get me. Without a word, without a question, without a moment's hesitation, they were there.

Back home, midway through *Mission Impossible,* as the theme music swelled and Phelps cut the wires on the Russian explosive in the nick of time, I slipped Daffodil off my lap and went to my room. I rifled through my pajama drawer and found my old Dr. Denton pj's, the kind with feet, stuffed deep in the drawer, tucked shamefully away, like a lunatic cousin...from Jacksonville, maybe.

I tried them on to see if they still fit. I *ached* for those footed pj's to fit. But no. No matter how hard I tried, they just didn't.

And then I realized: There is no going back.

There's no going back in our walk with God, either. Oh, we *can* go back, of course. But it doesn't suit us; it's no longer who we are. The old ways we used to live and the things we used to do don't fit who we are *becoming*. Jesus said that the new wine He's pouring into us just doesn't fit in the old wineskins; they'll burst (Matthew 9:17). The new life He gives us simply can't be contained in the old person, living in the old ways.

We don't always like it, and sometimes we may wrestle and wriggle and try to squeeze back into what used to fit us. But in His great love for us, God is intent on growing us up. He wants us to "become mature, attaining to the whole measure of the fullness of Christ...[that] we will in all things grow up into him who is the Head, that is, Christ" (Ephesians 4:13, 15). The Father's love for us is so great that He won't let us remain children.

Whether you're twelve or twenty-five or seventy, growing up is frightening. But there's no getting out of it and no going back. God calls us to grow and mature—and He promises to walk with us every step of the way. Through growing pains and uncertainty, changes and shock waves, when our world seems to fall apart, He never leaves us, never forsakes us. When we call on Him, He always picks us up and takes us home...without a word, without a question, without a moment's hesitation.

That's just what Love does.

Father, I admit that growing up—

growing in You—is often difficult and frightening.

I sometimes want to go back.

I don't want to go through the growing pains

of becoming the person You desire me to be.

But, Lord, thank You that You are

a patient and faithful Father.

Even when I try to wriggle out of growing into this new life

You've called me to, Your love won't let me.

Your wondrous love is determined

to grow me up, to make me like Your Son.

And all the while, You are there…

ever gentle, ever caring, ever faithful.

Amen

SHADOWED

LOVE

We fix our eyes not on what is seen,
but on what is unseen.
For what is seen is temporary,
but what is unseen is eternal.

2 CORINTHIANS 4:18

I REMEMBER A MORNING not so long ago when my life seemed to be crashing down—family crises, health concerns, infertility heartache, financial worries, a frustrating stall in my career. The California sun was shining through my bedroom window, but it felt like someone had drawn the shades. It was so very dark.

You've been there, too, haven't you?

Sometimes we are desperate to see God, but we can't because it's so dark. "We look for light, but all is darkness; for brightness, but we walk in deep shadows. Like the blind we grope along the wall, feeling our way like men without eyes" (Isaiah 59:9–10).

Have you been groping your way through dark places? Have you faced hardships or heartaches that have left you wondering, *Where are You, God? Are You even here? I can't see You!* Perhaps your life seems black as night, with no sliver of light, no ray of hope. But hold on! The mystery of God is that He dwells—and shows us His love—even in the dark.

Difficulties will come to all of us. God allows us to go through dark times and hard circumstances that fly in the face of our expectations, challenge our logic, drain our emotional energy, and make us want to give up. Some trials come because of sin—our own sins or those of others. Some are the work of the enemy of our soul, Satan. And some are simply due to the fact that we live in a fallen world.

When the trials come, we cry out, *But God, if You love me, how can You allow this in my life?* He answers, "I have allowed this in your life because I *do* love you."

In prayer that dark morning, I sensed Him whisper to my heart, "You aren't being punished; you are being *tested*. When I'm squeezing you in your circumstances, I'm actually squeezing you close to My heart. Think of it like a hug— when I squeeze you, I'm squeezing you tight to Me. Lean into Me, rest in Me, hold on to Me in the dark. Stop struggling, let Me hold you tight. I'll whisper what you need to know. Even if I do take everything, you still have Me. Isn't that enough? I'm going to squeeze you tight until that's enough."

Even if we've known God a long time, all too often we still try to walk by sight, not by faith. We see things through the eyes of our own understanding, not God's. So sometimes He has to turn out the lights. He hits the main breaker, plunges us into deep darkness, and then asks us to seek Him there.

Solomon wrote, "The LORD has said that he would dwell in a dark cloud" (1 Kings 8:12). God came in a cloud and revealed Himself to Moses. He said, "[I am] the compassionate and gracious God, slow to anger, abounding in love and faithfulness, maintaining love to thousands, and forgiving wickedness, rebellion and sin" (Exodus 34:6–7). God wants us to come to Him—not just for the blessings He gives, but for who He is. And He promises that if we seek Him, we will find Him. "Come near to God," the apostle James writes, "and he will come near to you" (James 4:8).

"Our God, the God of our fathers, is a hidden God," Stefan Zweig writes. "And not until we are bathed in sorrow are we enabled to discern Him."[3] In pain and struggle and difficulty, we see Him in ways we never have before. In the darkest night season, our eyes finally adjust and we begin to get a glimpse of His power and mercy and love. True faith is "being sure of what we hope for and certain of what we do not see" (Hebrews 11:1). Through all our difficult circumstances, God is leading us to have a faith like His friend Job, who said, "Though He slay me, yet will I trust Him" (Job 13:15, NKJV).

So even though I couldn't see or understand what God was doing during that dark time, I chose to trust Him. All alone, broken and bleeding, I lifted my head and opened the Book. Fumbling for comfort I was certain I wouldn't find…I found it. My eyes landed on the soaring climax to Peter's first letter: "And the God of all grace, who called you to his eternal glory in Christ, after you have suffered a little while, will himself restore you and make you strong, firm and steadfast" (1 Peter 5:10).

Oswald Chambers put it like this:

There are times, says Jesus, when God cannot lift the darkness from you, but trust Him. God will appear like an unkind friend, but He is not; He will appear like an unnatural Father, but He is not; He will appear like an unjust judge, but He is not. Keep the notion of the mind of God…strong and growing. Nothing happens in any particular unless God's will is behind it, therefore you can rest in perfect confidence in Him.[4]

During that shadowed season of my life—and in the dark seasons since—I relaxed in God's arms. I stopped groping along on my own, trying to squint my eyes to see. Instead, I began to search for Him in the darkness. And as I did, I caught a glimmer of one of the unseen mysteries of the spiritual life: Some of God's deepest truths and richest wonders are hidden in the darkest shadows.

God is sometimes in the darkness. And He sometimes asks us to enter the darkness, too; to be willing to go through the cloud to come to Him. And as we do, we see His mercy in uncertainty, His power in the dark clouds, His love in the shadows.

I thought again of Moses. Because he went into the dark cloud, he got to meet with God. "Then Moses entered the cloud as he went up on the mountain" (Exodus 24:18). Let's be willing to see God in all the loving ways He manifests Himself to us. Let's not be afraid to enter the cloud.

Lord, I want to know You more deeply.

I want to walk by faith, not just sight.

Help my eyes to adjust in the dark.

Reveal Yourself in these shadowy

depths in ways I've never known before.

I'm entering the cloud, Lord.

I want to see You,

I want to meet with You—even there.

Show me Your love and

faithfulness in the shadows.

Amen

TRUSTWORTHY

But I trust in your unfailing love;
my heart rejoices in your salvation.
I will sing to the LORD,
for he has been good to me.

PSALM 13:5–6

WHAT'S YOUR PICTURE OF
God? Is it hard for you to trust Him?

Shelley's father was an alcoholic. He abused her for years
while her mother seemed oblivious, and Shelley was too
ashamed to tell anyone. She trusted her father; he was supposed to protect and nurture her. But instead, the protector

became the perpetrator. As a result, Shelley had wounds etched deep, feelings of shame and pain and deep distrust.

How could she trust? *And how could she possibly trust God?* Where was He during those times when she felt anything but safe and protected and loved?

Shelley is grown up now and has come to faith in Christ. But it has taken many years for her to trust God completely. She just couldn't picture God as a safe, loving, trustworthy father.

Can you relate? If you have had painful experiences with a parent or another authority figure, if you've experienced abandonment, neglect, or physical, emotional, or sexual abuse, it may be very hard to see God as Protector and Friend. It may be difficult for you to place your future in His hands, a stretch to believe that He really loves you. The Bible says, "The one who was born of God keeps him safe, and the evil one cannot harm him" (1 John 5:18). You read a Scripture like this and shake your head in confusion. *Then just where* was *God during all those times in my life?*

Even if you haven't had horrific experiences like Shelley, you might still struggle with trusting God, with believing that His love for you is real. It may be hard to see Him as a God who adores you, delights in you, and wants to be close to you because He loves you with a pure and passionate love.

No matter what you have experienced, God did not abandon you. He did not ignore your cry for help. He was with you. And He is with you now.

Trust, of course, needs to be earned. After all, no one is truly trustworthy until put to the test. No one is worthy of our confidence until proven to be so. I think that's why over and over in His Word God tells us about Himself, reminds us of His character and nature, proves to us His steadfast faithfulness, and invites us to trust Him—based on His nature, not on our feelings or experiences. He invites us to test Him: "Taste and see that the LORD is good" (Psalm 34:8), and when we do, we find that God is indeed a loyal, devoted Friend. We find that He does love us—so much that He sent His own Son to die for us, so much that He became separated from Christ so that nothing could ever separate us from Him.

In Psalm 13, David speaks for all who have felt betrayed, abandoned, or abused, all who have asked God *why?* "How long, O LORD? Will you forget me forever? How long will you hide your face from me? How long must I wrestle with my thoughts and every day have sorrow in my heart?" (vv. 1–2). Yet, as he came to experience God as his fully dependable deliverer, King David wrote psalm after psalm about God's unfailing love.

In a testimony to the safety and security of all who trust in God, he wrote, "I will say of the LORD, 'He is my refuge and my fortress, my God, in whom I trust'" (91:2).

In a commitment of faith following the deliverance of Judah, he led the nation to proclaim: "He is our help and our shield. In him our hearts rejoice, for we trust in his holy name. May your unfailing love rest upon us, O LORD, even as we put our hope in you" (33:20–22).

In a reflection of God's unfailing protection, he wrote: "Your love, O LORD, reaches to the heavens, your faithfulness to the skies. Your righteousness is like the mighty mountains, your justice like the great deep…. How priceless is your unfailing love! Both high and low among men find refuge in the shadow of your wings" (36:5–7).

David concludes with words of resounding confidence in God, a testimony to the people of God's character and unfailing love in the midst of trials. "But I trust in your unfailing love; my heart rejoices in your salvation. I will sing to the LORD, for he has been good to me" (13:5–6).

That's what Shelley concluded, too. As she trusted God with her whole life, her present, future—and her past—He enabled her to overcome it. It didn't happen overnight. But as she opened her heart and asked God to increase her faith in Him, she has come to rely on Him more and more. And more and more she has seen the results of His faithfulness in her life.

Are you getting a clearer picture of this loving and trustworthy God?

God wants you to trust Him; He wants you to know Him as your faithful Father. He wants to remove from you anything that hinders you from entering into that kind of love and trust relationship with Him.

Take some time alone, and if you're able, think about

whatever experience has injured you, whatever memory still haunts you. Then, as best you can, place it in God's hands and ask His love to break its power over your life.

He will. For that's who He is. You can rest your very life in His care and keeping. And as you do, "May the God of hope fill you with all joy and peace as you trust in him" (Romans 15:13).

Father, I have not always had a clear picture of You.

Help me to see the truth—that I can trust You.

In the name of Jesus Christ,

break the power of any evil committed against me

and the negative effects that has had on me.

I place all these things that I have carried for so long

in my heart and mind into Your hands.

Cleanse me completely and help me to forgive.

Help me grasp the depth of Your love for me.

Remove anything that keeps me

from trusting You completely.

Amen

COMFORTING
LOVE

"As a mother comforts her child,
so will I comfort you."

ISAIAH 66:13

WHEN I WAS LITTLE, "IN
the Garden" was my mom's favorite hymn. Curled up in her
lap, my head squooshed into her pillow-soft chest, I would
rock with her in the brown nubby Ethan Allen rocker with
the box pleat ruffle and the tiny creak in the spring.

Through earaches, scraped knees, and monsters under
my bed, through schoolmate snubs, broken hearts, and
piano recital fiascoes, this was my balm. We would rock

together in the darkened living room, bathed in just a hint of a bluish light flickering from the TV room where Daddy was watching *The Ed Sullivan Show.* I don't remember if he even turned down the volume, but I couldn't have heard it anyway.

All I heard was her. Singing to me. And singing to Jesus.

Mom wasn't a good singer. But I didn't know that. I loved her voice, with its deep register, little rasp, and slight vibrato. But mostly I loved the feel of her voice and the softness and intimacy it produced as the sound rumbled from her chest. I didn't so much hear her as *feel* her; it wasn't how her voice sounded but how it felt that soothed and assured, healed and relaxed me.

Mom rocked me and sang that song until I was far too old for that kind of thing. When my toes touched the ground, I folded my long legs into her lap as far as possible, and when they got too long for that, I started using my own feet to keep us rocking. Then one day I realized that her strained singing and labored breathing wasn't from tender emotions, but from me crushing her lungs into her rib cage, squeezing the air right out of her. Both sad, we retired our ritual. But during all those years, rocking in Mom's lap, wrapped in her arms and nestled into her chest, I learned what God's love and comfort feels like.

I learned about "the Father of compassion and the God of all comfort, who comforts us in all our troubles, so that we can comfort those in any trouble with the comfort we ourselves have received from God" (2 Corinthians 1:3–4). I sensed the peace and power of the God who turns our "mourning into gladness" and gives us "comfort and joy instead of sorrow" (Jeremiah 31:13). And as I rocked on Mom's lap, I felt the blessing of Moses: "Let the beloved of the LORD rest secure in him, for he shields him all day long, and the one the LORD loves rests between his shoulders" (Deuteronomy 33:12).

Because I'd come to know the Father of compassion who comforts us in all our troubles, I found that I could hold a weeping woman in my arms after her miscarriage. Because I'd come to know the God who turns our mourning into gladness, I sensed His peace and power when my dad went home to heaven. Because as a child I had felt the blessing of Moses, I found confidence and rest when the security of our jobs was yanked away and our finances were strained. Because I'd come to know the God of all comfort, I continue to experience His comfort during times of uncertainty, failure, and disappointment.

Now, as an adult, I understand why "In the Garden" was Mom's favorite hymn. It has become mine, too. I had always thought those moments in her lap, rocking and singing, were just for me. Yes, certainly, they were Mom's gifts to me, of her time and her life, but I now believe that she was stealing precious moments for herself as well.

Who can know what Mom prayed for her daughter as she rocked her and stroked her back? Did she ever cry out,

I'm so tired…. I've given all I can give today. Just help her sleep, Lord! Did she ever ask, *What about me?* Ever tell the Lord, *I love my family, but what about my dreams, my talents, my hopes? Is this all You want me to do with all You've given me?* Did this strong, confident woman ever feel helpless to dress the wounds of her little one? Did she shed tears over my physical and emotional pain? Did she cry out to God for wisdom, patience, and love in rearing her child?

Whatever my mom's prayers were, I believe they were beautiful encounters between her and her Beloved. I imagine that as Mom rocked me and prayed for me, prayed for herself and for the grace to raise me, God met her in that garden…and walked with her, talked with her, and assured her she was His own. As she soothed her child, Love soothed His.

"Come away," He whispers to us…and draws us into quiet places where we can walk with Him and talk with Him and simply *be* with Him. He meets us in the garden and comforts us there with His love.

And we never get too old for this.

Father, You surround me with Your comfort

and overwhelm me with Your tenderness.

Thank You for Your gentle love,

which calms, soothes, and reassures me.

I know that whatever happens in my life,

I can rest in the shelter of Your loving arms.

Now, Lord, please use me to comfort others.

Help me to be sensitive to those around me

who need Your consoling touch.

Help me reach out to them with the same

loving comfort I have received from You.

Amen

DEMONSTRATIVE

OVE

God demonstrates his own love for us in this:
While we were still sinners, Christ died for us.

ROMANS 5:8

OD LOVES YOU."

We say those words to people in the midst of heartbreak, devastating circumstances, and crushing pain. We say the same thing to all of them:

To the expectant couple watching the fetal heart monitor flatline.

To the godly father of three children under five who is riddled with cancer.

To the newly abandoned single mom with no job skills or money.

To the child of parents mowed down by a drunk driver. *Words, words, words!*

Even for those who acknowledge the truth in them, there are shattering times when those words leave us cold and sound like nothing more than religious rote. At times like these, how can we *know* that God truly loves us?

Max Lucado says, "God answered our question before we asked it. So we'd see his answer, he lit the sky with a star. So we'd hear it, he filled the night with a choir; and so we'd believe it, he did what no man had ever dreamed. He became flesh and dwelt among us."[5]

God demonstrated His love for us in language we could understand.

Veiling His majesty, Jesus slipped into skin so that someday He could get under mine. He shed His glory, traversed time and space, and found a home in the womb of a teenage girl so that He could make His home in my heart.

God demonstrated His love for us by sending His Son to show us what the Father is like. "The Word became flesh and made his dwelling among us. We have seen his glory, the glory of the One and Only, who came from the Father, full of grace and truth" (John 1:14). As Jesus said, "Anyone who has seen me has seen the Father" (14:9).

God demonstrated His love for us by sending His Son to die in our place. "For God was pleased to have all his fullness dwell in him, and through him to reconcile to himself all things...by making peace through his blood, shed on the cross" (Colossians 1:19–20). Henry Wadsworth Longfellow said, "Not father or mother has loved you as God has.... When he bowed his head in the death hour, love solemnized its triumph."[6] Christ says to us:

I looked down from the cross. I thought of you.

They pierced My side. I thought of you.

They drove nails through My wrists. I thought of you.

I rose to new life. And I gave it to you.

And God demonstrated His love for us by sending His Son to show us how to love others. We do that the same way He did—by using language they can understand. Sometimes we use words, but we can also become "Jesus with skin on"—and do the same kind of things He did while He was on earth. Love should be our distinguishing mark, the obvious, unmistakable trait that makes us known.

Do you ever think about all the people who have blessed you throughout your life? The tireless teachers, generous relatives, and thoughtful neighbors? Some encouraged, some disciplined, some just listened. They took time out of their lives to love you. Sometimes it was gentle love; sometimes it was tough. Sometimes, frankly, it didn't feel so good—like the coach who wouldn't settle for your performance on the field, or Mrs. Horn, who wouldn't settle for mine on the piano. Maybe we didn't welcome their "input" at the time, but with the gracious gift of hindsight, today we can see how we benefited from their love. How grateful we are that they spoke to us in a language we could understand!

Life is about love. We are here to learn to love. And we do that by practicing on each other. It is in loving that we are most like Him, so love is His consistent command. "A new command I give you…" He said. "As I have loved you, so you must love one another. By this all men will know that you are my disciples, if you love one another" (John 13:34–35).

We're to be Jesus with skin on. That's what Love looks like.

Love looks like my dear friend Julaine, who brings nutritious, fresh-baked goodies to the gals in her office and insists on driving her office-mate, Claire, to all her chemo appointments. My housebound mom can't go to church anymore, so Julaine and her husband, Jimi, bring church to Mom. They sing worship songs, serve communion to her, and pray for her.

Love looks like our neighbor Tom, who donated a portion of his liver to save the life of a stranger.

And love looks like *you* when you deny yourself something you really want in order to encourage, bless, or help someone in real need.

When we say "God loves you" and then roll up our sleeves, or pull out our checkbook, or sacrifice our time and sweat and tears to *show* what love looks like, those in sorrow or deep crisis will begin to believe it.

Acts of kindness, great or small, costly sacrifices or considerate gestures, every time you do an act of lovingkindness, you're being Jesus with skin on to others. You are speaking a language they can understand. And God will magnify even the smallest of your deeds to demonstrate His great love to them.

Lord, I don't want to speak empty words

when I say to others, "God loves you."

I want them to see Your love in action through me.

Forgive me for being self-centered.

Move me out of my comfort zone.

Help me to be more generous and

thoughtful and sacrificial

in ways that will be most meaningful to others,

in ways that will reflect Your incredible love for them.

Help me to love as You love.

Amen

12

SECURE *Love*

Let the beloved of the LORD

rest secure in him.

DEUTERONOMY 33:12

ONE COLD AND BLUSTERY DAY, I was driving to our ranch in the mountains just north of Los Angeles. As I navigated the icy road a few miles from our house, I hit some black ice and skidded off the road. Fortunately I wasn't hurt, but the vehicle was stuck. I was in utter wilderness, and it was getting dark. Groping for my cell phone, I punched in my husband's number.

Larry's voice was calm. "Where are you? What's your position?"

Willing my voice to remain steady, I described my exact location. "I'm on the north side of the road, just east of Jane's ranch, between the sharp curve and the big stand of oak trees."

"Okay," he assured me. "Just sit tight. I'll be right there." And he was. Twenty minutes later I saw the welcome headlights of Larry's Jeep knifing through the darkness. He found me because I could pinpoint precisely where I was. And even as I waited alone in the cold and dark, I felt safe and secure because of that.

Just recently, a day-hiker in our area wasn't so fortunate. She got lost and had no idea which way to turn. Two days later, she was found dead from hypothermia, mere yards from the trail she'd been seeking. If only she had known her position, she would have been safe.

Have you ever wished you could feel so safe and secure that nothing—no circumstances, no person, no emotions—could ever shake you? Well, you can. Your security doesn't depend on something you have to continually *do*; it's something you already have, a place you already live.

It's your position in Christ:

We have this hope as an anchor for the soul, firm and secure. It enters the inner sanctuary behind the curtain, where Jesus, who went before us, has entered on our behalf.

HEBREWS 6:19–20

True security is anchored in God's love for us. Jesus reminds us: "As the Father has loved me, so have I loved you" (John 15:9). In His final petition to the Father, Jesus prayed for us. "I have made you known to them," He said, "and will continue to make you known in order that the love you have for me may be in them and that I myself may be in them" (17:26). Our security is the certainty of our position in Christ and the assurance of His love, whatever our circumstances.

You can rest secure in the knowledge that there is nothing you can do to make Jesus love you more, and there is nothing you can do to make Him love you less. He loves you...even if you don't always love yourself. When you grasp the fact that God loves you passionately, intensely, and unconditionally, when you live your life from the freedom of your position in Christ, you are truly secure. You are a child of the most high God and a joint heir with Christ; you are His bride and His beloved. You don't have to fear.

King Jehoshaphat once faced a vast army positioned against his tiny nation of Judah. The Israelites' only hope lay with God. As they sought the Lord together in a great national prayer meeting, the Spirit of the Lord came upon a Levite, Jahaziel, who prophesied to the king:

> "You will not have to fight this battle. Take up your positions; stand firm and see the deliverance the LORD will give you, O Judah and Jerusalem. Do not

be afraid; do not be discouraged. Go out to face them tomorrow, and the LORD will be with you."

2 CHRONICLES 20:17

And the Lord will be with you, too.

The calm, steady assurance of His mighty love will sustain us as we face trials, difficulties, and any number of "impossible" situations. So even when our circumstances seem dire—even when our finances evaporate, our relationships disintegrate, and we experience distress, disillusionment, and despair—we are secure. "Who shall separate us from the love of Christ?" Paul asks,

> Shall trouble or hardship or persecution or famine or nakedness or danger or sword? No, in all these things we are more than conquerors through him who loved us. For I am convinced that neither death nor life, neither angels nor demons, neither the present nor the future, nor any powers, neither height nor depth, nor anything else in all creation, will be able to separate us from the love of God that is in Christ Jesus our Lord.

ROMANS 8:35, 37–39

What would you add to that list? What event, circumstance, or situation could possibly drive a wedge between you and your Savior? Will personal failure, family heartaches, or prolonged depression? No! Will loneliness, grief, or loss? Never! Neither will infertility, bankruptcy, or terminal illness, nor fires or floods or terrorist atrocities. Nothing—but *nothing*—can separate us from the love of God that is in Christ Jesus!

As his army set out, King Jehoshaphat sent the worshipers ahead of them, singing praises as they went. The exhortation of that good king is for us as well: "Have faith in the LORD your God and you will be upheld…. 'Give thanks to the LORD, for his love endures forever'" (2 Chronicles 20:20–21).

In His love, your position is secure.

Thank You, Lord, that whatever

may happen in my life,

there is nothing that can separate me from You.

Your love establishes me, surrounds me,

and settles me at the core of my being.

I know beyond the shadow of a

doubt that I am Yours.

I am confident in Your love,

I do not have to fear,

I can rest, comfortable, secure, and free

in Your arms because my position

in You is unshakable!

Amen

13

GLORIOUS *Love*

God's glory is on tour in the skies,
God-craft on exhibit across the horizon.
Madame Day holds classes every morning,
Professor Night lectures each evening.
PSALM 19:1–2, *THE MESSAGE*

*I*T'S THE CRACK OF DAWN, and a symphony of birds wakens me. The melodies of songbirds, the rat-a-tat-tat of a woodpecker, the faint chirps of hungry babies waiting for breakfast. I open my eyes to the amber glow of the mountains just before sunrise. That jeweled rim of light along the ridge—a special gift to those who rise early before light breaks into day for the rest of the world to see. Slowly, slowly the color swells. Then the sun bursts over the mountains.

I'm at our Southern California ranch retreat, a beautiful place of refuge and tranquillity that my husband, Larry, and I created for people like us—and you—to slip away for a while from the rush and chaos and enjoy some much-needed solitude. It's a place where many come to dial down, get restored and refreshed, hear God's voice…and get to know Him again.

I pad barefoot onto the veranda and curl up in a rocker. A delicately scented breeze wafts through roses, jasmine, and the profusion of blooms on the buckeye tree. Huge gray squirrels, bushy tails bobbing, scamper up majestic pines to gather nuts from foot-long cones. Rabbits gaze longingly into my chicken-wired vegetable garden, hoping against hope to nab summer's first tomatoes and peppers.

The yard is alive with birds. Chartreuse finches, all ruffled feathers and high-pitched chirps, tentatively leave their nest behind the porch lantern to follow mom to the rock fountain for their first birdbath. A fat, round robin and an intensely vivid bluebird flit and dart, while an oriole perches atop the small sycamore tree, its yellow and black blazing against the clear azure sky. A hummingbird zips from wildflower to daylily. A mama quail scoots across the gravel drive and into the pasture, six babies in tow, their little legs a blur of speed.

Then stillness. Quiet. Deafening silence until an unseen

breeze causes the leaves in the balm of Gilead trees to shimmer and dance. Soft at first, just a whisper. Then those shimmering leaves swirl wildly as the sound rises. Now the wind rushes through the pines, and they join in—a deeper pitch. It builds until the whole forest roars a perfect chord with the unseen breeze.

And it's gone. Silence again.

Now I know what the prophet Isaiah meant when he said, "The mountains and hills will burst into song before you, and all the trees of the field will clap their hands" (Isaiah 55:12). The earth cannot help but sing and dance and cry out in joy and adoration of its Creator. The stillness shouts His glory. The deafening silence is filled with Him. The soft breeze caresses my cheek and neck. The warm sun melts my world-worn heart. I inhale the fragrance of His presence. He's closer than a breath, showing His love through creation itself. Supernatural reveals itself through the natural; the invisible through the visible.

Yet though He made it, He is not it. Creation is a signpost for Him—a breadcrumb He leaves us on the trail to His throne. C. S. Lewis wrote: "Because God created the Natural—invented it out of His love and artistry—it demands our reverence."[7] But he also said:

We must not try to find a direct path through it and beyond it to an increasing knowledge of God. The path peters out almost at once. Terrors and mysteries, the whole depth of God's counsels and the whole tangle of the history of the universe, choke it. We can't get through: not that way. We must make a *detour*—leave the hills and woods and go back to our studies, to church, to our Bibles, to our knees.[8]

Creation declares God's wonders, but the Cross declares His love. To understand and reciprocate His love, we must know Him through more than just His handiwork. We must know Him through what His Son has shown us and done for us, through what the Holy Spirit has revealed to us and deposited in us. We need to get to know Him. Because unless we know Him…we cannot possibly love Him.

When my friend Mary Ann was getting to know Christ she was worried.

"I don't really *love* Jesus," she said.

"Well, of course you don't," a wise friend replied. "You don't know Him. You couldn't possibly love *me* unless you got to know me, so how can you love Jesus unless you get to know Him?"

"Man's love of God," said Maimonides, "is identical with his knowledge of Him."[9] God invites us to get to know Him. He invites us to follow the breadcrumbs that lead to His love.

That morning at the ranch, curled up on the veranda, I marveled at the beauty of God's nature: "God's glory is on tour…God-craft on exhibit." And as "Madame Day" held class amidst the wonders of His creation, I drank in His beauty. I communed with Him in prayer, read His love letters, and allowed His Holy Spirit to whisper truths about Him through His Word. I got to know—and love—my Abba Father a little more. I followed the breadcrumbs to His glorious love.

Glorious King, Lord of all beauty,

Creator of heaven and earth,

I am in awe at the works of Your hand

and the wonders of Your great love.

Thank You for Your natural

splendor that surrounds me——

the sights and sounds and smells that delight me.

Jesus, You created all of it for

Your glory and our pleasure.

Your invisible love made visible,

a heavenly hint, a foretaste of Your glory,

that leads me to the cross…and Your throne.

Amen

AGONIZING
Love

We know that the whole creation has been groaning
as in the pains of childbirth right up to the present time.

ROMANS 8:22

ONCE, IN THE STILL OF
twilight with no one else around, I walked through the
Garden of Gethsemane.

Eight eerie sentinels stood guard in the gathering darkness. As ancient as Christianity itself, these enormous,
gnarled olive trees have been traced back two millennia to
that night of tears and blood, agony and betrayal.

I ran my hand along the bark of those twisted trees,

feeling the deep crevices, natural cisterns where creation's tears might have flowed. Those contorted trunks hold secrets that only heaven knows.

They were there that night. They were alive in His presence. *But did they know? Could they possibly have known?*

Paul writes to the Romans, "We know that the whole creation has been groaning as in the pains of childbirth right up to the present time" (8:22). What does the "whole of creation" include? Humans and angels, yes. But nature, too? Does it include the Garden of Gethsemane itself? Did those olive trees lament and writhe in protest? Was it grief that twisted those ancient trunks?

As I walked through the twilight grove, I pictured Peter and James and John dozing—just over there—unconscious to the cataclysmic events raging around them. Who would have known a cosmic struggle was underway? That eternity hung in the balance?

All alone, with no friends at His side, overwhelmed with sorrow to the point of death, Jesus pled for another way. Tears, torment, sweat like blood. A request. Must He, who had no sin, bear all sin? Must He, the spotless Lamb, be the final scapegoat? And the most piercing reality of all—must He, the eternal Son, be separated from His Father? Must this be?

No one really knows what transpired between Father and Son that night. No one can begin to understand how the human nature of the God-Man struggled alongside His divine nature. Did He remember a conversation within the Trinity, somewhere in eternity past? Did He recall devising a plan—a glorious act of love—to rescue a lost and fallen creation? Did He think of His friends and their eternal destiny in that moment? Did He see your face…and mine?

If it had been me in those desperate hours, I would have wondered, *Are they worth it?* Everything in my humanness would long to live, escape the pain, shrink away from the horror of death and separation.

Perhaps His Father reminded Him of the prayer He had just offered on behalf of His followers: "I will remain in the world no longer, but they are still in the world, and I am coming to you.… For them I sanctify myself, that they too may be truly sanctified" (John 17:11, 19). Immediately after that prayer, Jesus went to the Garden of Gethsemane.

There He fell at the base of the olive trees—those silent witnesses—in grief and anguish. And He made His choice. As He drank that cup of sorrow and suffering, He said, "Yes, Father, Your will be done." The holy bargain was struck. His life for ours. The Creator of all exchanged for the created. And there in the Garden on that night of nights, all nature joined in the groan over what had to be. A mournful dirge sounded in heaven and echoed throughout creation.

They knew. They had to have known. Just as the skies knew and would turn dark as He hung on the cross. Just as the earth knew and would shudder and convulse when He gave up His spirit. The trees knew. And they twisted and writhed in the Garden.

But anguish would soon turn to triumph. Christ's agony on the cross would become victory. Because of Jesus' decision that night in the Garden, "in him we have redemption through his blood, the forgiveness of sins" (Ephesians 1:7). Paul assures us that before the creation of the world—even before that other garden, Eden—God had chosen us for Himself. Because of Christ, we are adopted into His family as His own sons and daughters. Through Christ, He fulfilled His "long-range plan in which everything would be brought together and summed up in him, everything in deepest heaven, everything on planet earth" (Ephesians 1:10, *The Message*).

And yet we still groan—a deep moan, like the pains of childbirth. A mix of frustration and eager expectation stirs in our hearts as we await that day when all living things will be free from death and destruction. And Paul tells us that, whether we know it or not, "we ourselves, who have the first-fruits of the Spirit, groan inwardly" (Romans 8:23). We join all of creation in groans of both burden and hope—longing for that day of resurrection, when we will be "clothed with our heavenly dwelling," yearning for that day when He will come again (2 Corinthians 5:4).

Until then, we have a Comforter, the Holy Spirit, who has been sent to help us. When we do not know what we ought to pray for, the Spirit helps us in our weakness, interceding for us "with groans that words cannot express" (Romans 8:26).

Those ancient olive trees in Gethsemane that groaned in agony for Christ are not alone. All of nature, God, and man are groaning as one, waiting in eager anticipation for all things to come together.

For the sons of God to be revealed.

For Love to make all things new in heaven and earth.

Father, I can only imagine the agony of

Your Son that night in Gethsemane.

What unfathomable love to endure such torment!

Jesus, thank You for saying yes in that garden

and for suffering and dying on the cross

so that I would have life.

Thank You for Your Holy Spirit,

who comes alongside and helps me.

My anticipation deepens, Lord, for that day when

Your glory will be revealed in all of creation

and all will be made new.

Amen

FREE LOVE

"I will heal their waywardness
and love them freely."

HOSEA 14:4

ON'T HURRY TOO QUICKLY past that little verse tucked into the short book of Hosea. Within those nine simple words is the revelation of the whole of God's nature expressed through the Father, Son, and Holy Spirit—the "body of divinity in miniature," as Spurgeon calls it.[10]

It is what theologians have pondered and pilgrims have proclaimed.

And all who truly grasp it marvel at the wonder of His love.

God gave Adam and Eve a perfect Garden overflowing with delights and told them they could eat *freely* from all the plants…save one. "You must not eat from the tree of the knowledge of good and evil," God told them, "for when you eat of it you will surely die" (Genesis 2:17). But the crafty serpent slithered over to the woman and hissed, "You will not surely die.… For God knows that when you eat of it your eyes will be opened, and you will be like God, knowing good and evil" (3:4–5).

I can just imagine what ran through our first mother's mind as she chatted with the serpent beneath that tree. *Why, this is the very thing my man and I need to be satisfied, happy, and fulfilled! God says He loves us, so why can't we have it? He must be holding out on us. We'll just do it our own way.*

And they did. They believed Satan instead of God and ate the fruit.

Yet God's extravagant love could not be swayed. In lov-ingkindness, He sacrificed an animal to cover their sin and made garments from the skin to cover their shame. Then He announced a way of deliverance, a rescue plan formulated within the Godhead in eternity past—a design by which the woman's offspring would one day crush the serpent's head. God gave His people another chance.

God promised Abraham and his descendants a land flowing with milk and honey, and He Himself led the

Israelites out of slavery, through the wilderness, and on to the Promised Land. He rolled back the Red Sea for them, rained down manna to sustain them, and gave them a cloud and fire to direct them.

But somehow, it just wasn't enough.

Hungering for the delicacies of Egypt, they grew impatient and grumbled. *God says He loves us, so why is this taking so long? He must be holding out on us. We'll just do it our own way.*

And they did. They made their own golden calf and worshipped it instead of God.

Even so, "the LORD relented and did not bring on his people the disaster he had threatened" (Exodus 32:14). Centuries later, He would declare through His prophet, "I will heal their waywardness and love them freely…. I will betroth you to me forever; I will betroth you in righteousness and justice, in love and compassion. I will betroth you in faithfulness, and you will acknowledge the LORD" (Hosea 14:4; 2:19–20). And He gave His people yet another chance.

God loves to give His people another chance, a new beginning. And all the chances in the Old Testament were leading up to what is, in essence, our final chance, our ultimate opportunity. Because He loved us so immensely, God sent His own Son, who freely gave up everything He had—including His life—to heal our waywardness and redeem us.

We all have sinned and fallen short of His glorious ideal

for us, yet God has mercy on us, and "he will *freely* pardon" (Isaiah 55:7). Through Christ, we are "justified *freely* by his grace" (Romans 3:24). In the Son, God shouts His divine verdict of "Not guilty!" from the heavens. This is a love we don't deserve and could never earn. If we could, it wouldn't be free. This is a love streaming from heaven that confounds our every attempt to grasp it.

Knowing our struggle to comprehend, God freely pours out more of Himself through the Holy Spirit—even when we disbelieve, disobey, do our own thing, and go our own way. The Comforter woos us and assures us of God's love flowing freely toward us.

"But, Lord, I don't feel You. My heart is so cold."

That's not a requirement. My love has no conditions. I love you freely.

"But I fail again and again. I don't deserve Your forgiveness."

Of course you don't, but My grace through My Son is free to all, without merit on your part and without reservation on Mine. I love you freely.

"But, Lord, sometimes I think You're holding out on me. I'm not even sure I love You."

The offer stands. I will love you freely.

Whispering such assurances, the Holy Spirit both breaks and melts our hearts. He draws the wayward, the prodigal, and the skeptic home with the very words written centuries ago to a nation of backsliders: "I will heal their waywardness and love them freely, for my anger has turned away from them" (Hosea 14:4).

No penalty extracted. No fine levied. No payback required.

And then He stifles our objections with the kisses of His lips and "kill[s] our doubts by the closeness of His embrace."[11]

The great Alpha and Omega continues to invite the children of Adam and Eve to come into His presence, into His home, into His wondrous, eternal embrace. And He who has given everything, withholding nothing, will continue calling until the final darkness falls over this age and the eternal morning begins.

Come, receive My love. Freely.

Gracious Father, Your love is unlike

any love I've ever known.

Thank You that no matter what I have done,

You've given me a second chance—and a third

and a fourth—through Jesus.

Even now, when I stumble and fall,

You race toward me, freely offering

Your love and forgiveness.

I accept Your invitation to fall into Your arms

and freely drink in Your love and acceptance.

Amen

RECEIVING LOVE

"Freely you have received, freely give."

MATTHEW 10:8

W HEN WE THINK OF expressions of love, most of us agree with the words of Christ, quoted by Paul, that "It is more blessed to give than to receive" (Acts 20:35). These words notwithstanding, in the equation of love, *receiving* is just as important as giving. Love is, indeed, about giving. But as someone once said, "You can't give what you don't have."

Receiving is one of the native dialects of love.

On another occasion, when Paul said good-bye to the believers at Philippi, he told them that they were the only ones who had been generous with him and shared with him in "the matter of giving and receiving" (4:15). He made it abundantly clear that he wasn't looking for a gift; rather, he saw their giving as something that would be credited to their spiritual account. He knew that the investment value of their gifts wasn't so much what *he* would receive, but rather the "spiritual dividends" *they* would receive.

Okay, my head is spinning. I know it feels like we're talking to my accountant. But stay with me…this is one of the marvels of God's love.

You see, Paul understood one of the great wonders of love: that in order to give, he first had to receive.

God's economy of love is an endless cycle that begins with God giving and us receiving. Then, in turn, as we give to others from what we have received, He receives it as a gift to Himself. Jesus said, "Whatever you did for one of the least of these brothers of mine, you did for me" (Matthew 25:40). And then He credits it to our heavenly account, promising to meet all our needs "according to his glorious riches in Christ Jesus" (Philippians 4:19).

Think about it: What do we have that we did not receive from God? Nothing.

And what do we have that we did receive from Him? Everything.

- The kingdom (Mark 10:15)
- The Holy Spirit (John 20:22)
- Forgiveness (Acts 10:43)
- Grace (Romans 1:5)
- Comfort (2 Corinthians 1:3)
- Mercy (2 Corinthians 4:1)
- Eternal life (1 Timothy 1:16)

In Christ, God has committed *all* the riches of heaven to us. He holds them out, freely offering them to us, and we can choose whether or not to receive them. Some people choose not to. Jesus offered the Jews the gift of life. He told them that He was the Bread of Life and that whoever ate this bread would live forever. The disciple John tells us that many of Jesus' followers refused to receive this gift. "This is a hard teaching," they said. "Who can accept it?" (John 6:60). The choice was theirs to make, and "many of his disciples turned back and no longer followed him" (v. 66).

The Bible says that "anyone who will not receive the kingdom of God like a little child will never enter it" (Mark 10:15). But if we choose to receive His gift of love, God will also receive us to glory (Psalm 73:24).

When we begin to grasp the perfect, complete love God has for us, when we see that our own cup is full and overflowing, we can begin to look beyond ourselves and our needs—and look to others. Giving is easy when we truly recognize all that God has given to us. There is no need for us to withhold acceptance, affirmation, and encouragement from another for fear of not having enough of it ourselves.

And receiving from others becomes easy as well. We can appreciate the gifts and talents they possess. We aren't threatened by their beauty or success. There are no barriers, no walls we need to build up for protection. We can celebrate others' accomplishments, prosperity, and blessings untainted by our own insecurities and needs because we are secure in the fact that God will supply all that we truly need in His perfect time and perfect way.

There is such freedom in loving God and others this way! When we know who we are in Christ, we are completely confident. We truly fall in love with Jesus and serve Him and others for the right reasons—out of love. Not for attention, not to feel important or necessary, not to feel better about ourselves because we're doing lots of "good" deeds and "spiritual" activities, not to look good to the world or to gain the acceptance of God or others. Rather, our attention is so focused on Christ that what we do is simply an overflow of our love for Him.

God created us to be lovers. As we spend time with our Beloved, as we steal away to the secret place with Him and receive His affection, as He saturates us with His love and communicates His passion for us, that same love flows back through us to Him. As we receive His love and love Him back, the Father's love for Jesus flows back to Him—through us. What a wonder!

I think perhaps one day, when we stand before Him, our Beloved will ask us something about this matter of love. He will not likely ask how successful we were in men's eyes, how good our intentions were, or even how much "work" we did for Him. I think He will say to us, "I loved you freely. Did you receive it? Did you freely give it to others?"

Receive the love of God, embrace it, soak in it…then give to others—freely!

Lord, all that You had You gave to Jesus—

and He received it.

All that Jesus had He gives to me—

and I receive it.

All that I have in You,

help me give to others—and help them to receive it.

I marvel at Your divine economy of love—

that as I allow You to love others through me,

You credit it to my heavenly account.

So I joyously receive—and give—Your love freely!

Amen

FARSIGHTED

OVE

"For I know the plans I have for you,"
declares the LORD.

JEREMIAH 29:11

WAS SIX WHEN I GOT MY first pair of glasses.

When the ophthalmologist slipped them on my nose, I could hardly believe my eyes. That moment opened up a whole new world for me. For the first time, I could read all the lines on his chart. I could read the big letter E. I could read the next line and the next, and even the little bitty line on the bottom—FAXTHUPZ.

On the drive home, I was in a state of euphoria. "You mean there are individual leaves on the trees? Look…there are strings between the telephone poles. Daddy, watch out, there's a dog running across the street! I've never seen *that* before!"

I'm nearsighted. Without glasses, I can't see very far. But unlike me, God is farsighted. If I didn't know better (and I do), I might conclude that God is so farsighted that He can't even see what's right in front of His face. Things so obvious that even *I* could see them—*without* my glasses.

If God could see up close, surely He would have seen that Zacchaeus, hunkering in the sycamore tree, shading his shifty eyes, was a thief. He would have seen that Rahab, living in the house built over the gap between the walls of Jericho, was a harlot. He would have seen that Saul of Tarsus, persecuting and tormenting the followers of His Son, was His archenemy. And surely He would have seen that Nancy Stafford, dabbling in mysticism and bowing to the idols of materialism, self-centeredness, and sensuality, was a hopeless pagan.

Surely He could see all that. He's God. God sees everything, right? Right. But God doesn't see us as others do. In His love, He chooses to see who we will *become,* not who we have been.

When God looked at Zacchaeus, He saw a man as small in spirit as he was in stature, yet so desperate for love that he would go to any length—or height—to catch a glimpse of

Jesus. In Zacchaeus, He saw the perfect picture of repentance—a man so changed by Love that he withheld nothing and then lavished on others the love he had received.

When God looked at Rahab, He saw not a hardened prostitute, but His precious daughter. He saw strength, courage, and a radiant virtue that *He* would bestow on her. And looking down the long years with that far sight of His, He saw Rahab as the great-great-grandmother of King David, the woman from whose line His own Son, Jesus, would one day be born.

When God looked at Saul the persecutor, He saw Paul the evangelist. Inside this man consumed by hate, He saw a man who would be consumed with passion for His Son and the author of many of God's greatest love letters to the church.

And when God looked at me, He saw through my picture-perfect exterior, my illusion of confidence and happiness. He heard my silent scream of desperation, and He came near. He held out His hand and wiped my tears; He burned the idols of my life in the fire of His love. In me He saw a woman, broken and available, who would one day share with others, as best she could, the wonder of her Lord's transforming love.

I'd say God is pretty farsighted, wouldn't you?

God has grace-filled, long-range vision. Once we're forgiven, He chooses—no, He promises—to put our sins out of His sight forever: "Their sins and lawless acts I will remember no more" (Hebrews 10:17). He sees into the distance and focuses on our glorious future.

I didn't deserve to be chosen for such lavish, farsighted love. Neither did Zacchaeus or Rahab or Saul. Neither did you. No one deserves it. It is a gift—one that God freely offers to everyone. And He is just as committed to saving others as He was to rescuing us. No matter what people have done, God loves them—so much that He died for them.

He died for the parent who abandoned you.

He died for the husband who betrayed you.

He died for the boss who disappointed you.

He died for your best friends and your worst enemies.

He died for all of them as much as He died for you. Who knows what future He sees for them? Who knows what they will become in Christ?

Sometimes, even with my glasses on, I can still be very nearsighted. I can focus on the pettiest details, the smallest snubs, the tiniest offenses. I can put the flaws of others under my Coke-bottle-thick lenses and scrutinize them. But just as God doesn't focus on our imperfections, we shouldn't focus on the flaws of others. This doesn't mean that we're blind to the wrongs people commit or that we live in a state of denial. It simply means we choose to love so much that we take the long view of others' faults and failures.

After all, we really don't know what is in their hearts, do we? We don't know their intentions, and we can't fully understand their past, their pain, or their problems. But we can, lovingly and graciously, extend to them the same benefit we've received from God. As Paul writes: "After all, who are you to criticize the servant of somebody else, especially when that somebody is God?" (Romans 14:4, Phillips).

God's love sees far beyond what we might consider glaring imperfections. "Love is never so blind as when it is to spy faults," wrote seventeenth-century Anglican preacher Robert South. He said it's like the painter, who, when he paints a portrait of a friend with an imperfection, pictures only the other side of his face. "It is a noble and great thing to cover the blemishes and to excuse the failings of a friend; to draw a curtain before his stains, and to display his perfections; to bury his weaknesses in silence, but to proclaim his virtues upon the house-top."[12]

When we truly love, that's the way we'll see it.

After all, that's the way Love sees us.

Father, thank You that You

see far beyond just today—

and all the way into eternity.

You know the plans You have for me.

I pray that everything I do will move me toward

Your vision for me.

Help me become the person You intend for me to be.

Give me Your grace-filled eyes to see others.

Help me to overlook offense

and be blind to shortcomings.

Help me see others with eyes of love

and grace...just as You see me.

Amen

RENEWING

OVE

Do not conform any longer to the pattern of this world,
but be transformed by the renewing of your mind.

ROMANS 12:2

I'M READING THROUGH THE
book of Isaiah. So today I pulled my *Parallel Bible* from the
shelf and opened to the passage where I left off yesterday. My
eyes fell on the NIV translation, my favorite, and I began
reading Isaiah 53, the great prophetic chapter about our
Lord's identity and purpose.

I've read this passage many times. But this time the Holy
Spirit slowed my headlong rush. *Don't run through it because*

it's familiar to you, He whispered. *Read it as if for the first time.* I got only as far as verse 3: "He was despised and rejected by men."

O Lord, dear, precious Friend, how could they despise You? How could they reject the absolute love and complete freedom You came to give them? How could they?

Then my eyes fell on verse 3 in the King James Version: "He is despised and rejected of men." My heart stopped cold. *Is.* Present tense. He *is* despised and rejected. My eyes stung, and through tears I realized that Jesus was despised and rejected by *me. I despised You. I rejected You.* And the harder truth yet is that I often still do. I do it every time I care more about what the world thinks of me than what He thinks of me. I do it every time I believe negative thoughts or lies about who I am instead of believing the truth of who He says I am in Him.

The redemptive work of Christ is a reality, but its power to change us is in our minds. We're transformed by changing our thinking, renewing our minds. "Don't copy the behavior and customs of this world," Paul writes, "but let God transform you into a new person by changing the way you think" (Romans 12:2, NLT).

How do we renew the way we think? Oswald Chambers said, "I have to construct with patience the way of thinking that is exactly in accordance with my Lord. God will not make me think like Jesus, I have to do it myself."[13] Paul gives us the strategy: "We demolish arguments and every pretension that sets itself up against the knowledge of God, and we take captive every thought to make it obedient to Christ" (2 Corinthians 10:5).

Our divine weapon is the Word of God; the truth of Scripture is our sword of the Spirit. And Jesus shows us how to wield it. Following Jesus' baptism, the Spirit led Him into the desert, where Satan tempted Him. Each temptation was the enemy's effort to discredit His identity, derail Him from His destiny, and diminish His inheritance.

Each time Satan tempted Him, Jesus responded with "It is written." In Matthew 4:4, He says: "It is written: 'Man does not live on bread alone, but on every word that comes from the mouth of God.'" The Greek for *word* here is *rhema*, which means a spoken word. Jesus didn't use the word *logos*, which refers to the Scriptures as a whole, but rhema, the particular word a believer wields like a sword in the time of need. Rhema—the Word of God spoken out loud—is our chief weapon during our own struggles against Satan. When he tries to discredit our identity in Christ, derail us from our destiny, and make us doubt our inheritance, we're to respond with "It is written" and, like Jesus, declare a specific truth from Scripture.

We replace the tempter's lies with divine truth. We tear down every obstacle that keeps us from thinking the way God thinks, from having His viewpoint, from agreeing with Him about who He is and who we are in Him. We ruthlessly eliminate every thought that keeps us in bondage to our old ways of thinking. We take prisoner every thought that tries to take us prisoner, every shame and doubt, every accusation, every rejection and ridicule. Everything that hinders us from walking in the freedom of our true identity in Christ—we take it captive.

So when the old tapes play—*"I'm so stupid," "I knew I'd never do that right," "I'm hopeless"*—we say, "What? No way! You're under arrest! The Lord of the universe, the King of kings, has broken your power *and* given me authority over you. So I'm taking you captive, locking you up, and throwing away the key. The Bible says I am a new creation in Christ and accepted in the Beloved. He has redeemed my past and separated my sins from me forever. He's chosen me, delights in me, and given me a new name. It is written!"

When we read and believe the Word of God, it gets into our heart and soul and changes our thinking. A physician friend tells me that when we meditate upon God's Word, it uplifts and energizes us. Something actually happens in our body: Serotonin and dopamine levels rise, and our depression lifts. We feel better and want to do the things we didn't feel like doing before. We begin functioning and succeeding at a higher level. We feel confident. And we start seeing ourselves the way God sees us.

Renewing our minds with the truth of who we are in Christ is not a selfish act. Believing lies is what keeps us focused on ourselves. I'm sad to say that more than once in my life, my mind has been focused on what other people thought of me. A lot of us live like that—imprisoned and shackled by our thoughts.

But I've learned something. As someone once said: "What the world thinks of me is none of my business." My business—my privilege—is to renew my mind daily with what God thinks about me. And as I look once more at Isaiah 53:3, I determine to never again despise and reject Him by despising and rejecting myself.

The wonder of God's love is that in Christ we are redeemed, accepted, and free. Don't run past that thought because it's familiar to you. Hear it as if for the first time, as if He were speaking it to you this very moment.

Because He is.

Lord, I forget that when I

despise and diminish myself,

I despise and diminish Your work on the cross.

Forgive me!

You took my sin and past and

exchanged my life for Yours.

You changed me;

now help me change my thinking,

to take up the weapon of Your Word

against the lies that still plague me.

Help me to renew my mind with Your truth daily.

I have a new identity—You say so—

I am chosen, accepted, and deeply loved!

Amen

TRANSFORMING

OVE

We, who with unveiled faces all reflect the Lord's glory,
are being transformed into his likeness
with ever-increasing glory.

2 CORINTHIANS 3:18

OVE ISN'T SATISFIED WITH
simply renewing our thinking; He desires to transform our
very being, to conform us to His image.

When I first came to faith in Christ, I thought I was a
pretty good person already; I just needed salvation to get to
heaven. *I'm okay otherwise*, I thought. *I'm nice, thoughtful,*
easygoing; I don't party too much or do anything illegal.

Little did I know how much transforming I really needed! I didn't realize how self-centered and vain I really was. But as I got to know Jesus, as we built a relationship of abiding together, as I began to love Him and want to obey Him in everything, He began to change me.

In lovingkindness, God draws us to Him. He lifts us out of our sin and into new life. And then, as we allow Him to, He transforms us into the person He wants us to be. He replaces our old thoughts and beliefs with His truth, and that, in turn, changes our old ways of living and behaving.

The apostle Paul tells us that since we have died with Christ, died to the values of this world, since we have been "raised with Christ" and our "life is now hidden with Christ in God" (Colossians 3:1, 3), the way we used to live no longer suits us. "That isn't what you were taught when you learned about Christ," He reminds us (Ephesians 4:20, NLT). From Him we learn how we're to live. Therefore:

> Throw off your old evil nature and your former way of life, which is rotten through and through, full of lust and deception. Instead, there must be a spiritual renewal of your thoughts and attitudes. You must display a new nature because you are a new person, created in God's likeness—righteous, holy, and true.

VV. 22–24, NLT

We are a new creation; we have a new life in Christ. And so Paul gives us a new imperative: Live like it! "Put to death, therefore, whatever belongs to your earthly nature: sexual immorality, impurity, lust, evil desires and greed" (Colossians 3:5). The imagery is that of taking off an old, filthy garment covered with all those things that used to characterize us, including anger, rage, malice, slander, filthy language, and lies.

Instead, we slip into our new self, the one that Love is transforming into His likeness. "As God's chosen people, holy and dearly loved," Paul says, "clothe yourselves with compassion, kindness, humility, gentleness and patience. And over all these virtues put on love, which binds them all together in perfect unity" (Colossians 3:12, 14).

We're no longer to do anything out of selfish ambition, vanity, or conceit. We're to walk in humility toward others and in obedience to Christ. We look again to Love's example: Our attitude should be that of Christ, who "humbled himself and became obedient to death—even death on a cross!" (Philippians 2:8). The King of kings set aside His glory, put on skin, and made Himself nothing. In obedience to the Father, the Creator of all things became the servant of those He created.

Humility and obedience are the hallmarks of Christian character, the habits of behavior God uses to transform us into the image of His Son. "Love one another with brotherly affection. Outdo one another in showing honor," says Paul

(Romans 12:10, ESV). The NIV says it this way: "Honor one another above yourselves."

Then in verses 12 through 21, Paul gives us a character checklist:

- Hate what is evil; love what is good.
- Be joyful in hope, patient in hard times, constant in prayer.
- Share with those in need; practice hospitality.
- Bless your enemies; don't curse them.
- Rejoice with those who rejoice; weep with those who weep.
- Live in harmony with each other; don't repay evil for evil.
- Be friends with people of low position; don't be proud or conceited.
- As best you can, get along with everyone; overcome evil with good.

None of us are born with character; it has to be formed in us. Even Jesus learned obedience (Hebrews 5:8). Nor are we born with habits. We have to form them out of the common stuff of ordinary life.

"Drudgery is the touchstone of character," Oswald Chambers wrote. "The great hindrance in spiritual life is that we will look for big things to do. 'Jesus took a towel…and began to wash the disciples' feet.'" Chambers says the secret of our transformation is to respond to the tiniest task with humility and obedience and to learn to live in the "domain of drudgery" by the power of God. "Routine is God's way of saving us between our times of inspiration. The tiniest detail in which I obey has all the omnipotent power of the grace of God behind it."[14]

The word Paul used for *obedience* literally means attentive listening, with compliant submission and agreement. Obedience is simply agreeing with what God says and complying with His wishes—and doing it immediately. But I think this kind of obedience is possible only when we have the desire to obey because of our relationship with Christ. Power may achieve obedience, but only love can melt the heart. When the love is vibrant and active, obedience becomes, as one man describes it, a "dignity and delight."

When we believe and obey, we build a relationship that abides. "If you keep My commandments, you will abide in My love, just as I have kept My Father's commandments and abide in His love. This is My commandment, that you love one another as I have loved you" (John 15:10, 12, NKJV).

I'm reminded of an old saying: "When the heart weeps for what it has lost, the spirit laughs for what it has found." Strapping on the towel, bending down, and serving and loving out of humility and obedience changes us forever. And as we are transformed—as we die to self-centered, ambitious, vain pursuits—God will cause His love to flow through us to transform others.

Lord, I want to obey You in everything.

I want to please You and delight You.

Make me the person You want me to be.

Conform me to Your image, build my character,

and show me the habits, attitudes,

and behaviors I need to discard

and the attributes I need to adopt.

Transform me so You can use me

and love others through me.

Amen

RELINQUISHING *LOVE*

You know how full of love and
kindness our Lord Jesus Christ was.
Though he was very rich,
yet for your sakes he became poor,
so that by his poverty he could make you rich.

2 CORINTHIANS 8:9, NLT

RECENTLY, I COMPLETELY emptied out our self-storage unit and took a trailer-load of stuff to Goodwill. Although I had never subscribed to the material- istic mantra that whoever dies with the most possessions wins,

I had done my share of stockpiling over the years.

When I moved from Ft. Lauderdale to New York City to model and act, my stuff sat in storage until I had an unfurnished apartment and could surround myself with my stuff again. Then I moved from New York to L.A. My apartment was smaller than the one I'd had on the East Coast, so again, lots of my stuff went into storage. When I moved from the valley to the beach, some of my stuff didn't really suit that lifestyle, so it went into storage. Then I got married. Larry had been living on a sailboat, and since his stuff didn't fit onboard, he had put it in storage. With our marriage, two orange self-storage units became one.

As I hoisted box after box out of the trailer, I thought about all the time and energy and money I'd spent hanging on to stuff—things like the green sofa-bed that weighed a ton and never matched anywhere I ever lived, even though I did get it on sale and it was a steal. Watching it disappear into Goodwill, I did a quick calculation in my head. My $250 bargain had probably cost me close to $10,000 in storage fees over the past twenty years.

What's wrong with me? I wondered. Then as I drove home, I noticed for the first time how many orange self-storage units were strung along the highway. *What's wrong with us?* I wondered.

Long before storage buildings lined the freeways, psychoanalyst Erich Fromm posed the question, "If I am what I have, and what I have is lost, who then am I?"[15]

Professor Russell Belk of the University of Utah, who studies possessiveness and materialism, says that we have an impulse to acquire and keep things because our possessions remind us of who we are. If we lose our stuff, we feel somehow diminished; when it's gone, we fear, so are we.[16]

Despite what our culture tells us, accumulating more and more isn't the way to feel better about ourselves. How mistaken we are when we look for our identity in our appliances and furniture, in our cars and clothing! The truth is that a continual lust for more of anything in this world indicates we've forgotten that God is the source of our true identity.

Jesus' attitude toward storing up earthly goods is clear:

> "Do not store up for yourselves treasures on earth, where moth and rust destroy, and where thieves break in and steal. But store up for yourselves treasures in heaven, where moth and rust do not destroy, and where thieves do not break in and steal."
>
> Matthew 6:19–20

The next verse holds the key: "For where your treasure is, there your heart will be also" (v. 21).

Jesus is concerned about where our hearts are. He's concerned about what we love. He's concerned about our true home and our true identity.

When we forget who we are, we hang on and hoard and

store stuff we don't even need—even if it weighs us down and costs us. As I cleaned out my storage unit, I wondered how much other "stuff" I was hanging on to that I no longer needed. How much pain and bitterness—how much clutter—was I storing in my heart that was costing me dearly? And all of a sudden, relinquishing each item became an act of worship.

A pile of baskets became an offering of bad habits I had woven into my life; my old clothes became symbols of my self-righteousness; and the set of weights represented the unforgivingness that weighed me down. As I dropped off the treadmill, I determined to step off the one in my own life. As I gave up an old warped table, I gave up my warped self-perceptions. As I yielded each earthly "treasure" I had thought I could never live without, I yielded my pride, materialism, and fear.

Handing over the boxes became more and more exhilarating. I no longer reluctantly picked through my stuff; I handed it over faster and faster. "Take this, and this, and *please* take this, and I definitely don't want that anymore."

As I willingly relinquished all these things to God, I began to think, *What has God willingly given up for us?* And then I was struck: The answer is that He has relinquished everything. God Himself left the glory of heaven, humbled Himself, and came to earth as a man to die on a cross for us. He had treasures here He loved, so this is where His heart was. He still has treasures here, and He will not rest until He has redeemed them all. *We* are the possessions that He will never relinquish.

God loves us so much that He has given us treasures far better than anything we could store up for ourselves on earth. He has given us "a rich store of salvation and wisdom and knowledge" (Isaiah 33:6). These are the only kinds of possessions that can remind us who we really are. We don't need to store up things for ourselves here, because in His overflowing love, God does it for us. "Your goodness is so great! You have stored up great blessings for those who honor you. You have done so much for those who come to you for protection, blessing them before the watching world" (Psalm 31:19, NLT).

My stuff has never been of more value to me than it was the day I handed it over to the Lord, my Life, my Love, my True Identity. As I drove away, my storage unit was completely empty, but my treasures in heaven were overflowing. And then I realized—that is where my heart is.

Lord, show me the things I have stored inside

that clutter my heart or still give me my identity——

attitudes, fears, unforgivingness, idols.

Reveal to me those things I may be holding

on to that I love more than You.

Help me relinquish them all to You now——

I don't need them anymore! I only need You.

I love You, my Lord. You——and You alone——

are where my heart and my treasure lie.

Amen

WOUNDING LOVE

He was pierced for our transgressions,
he was crushed for our iniquities;
the punishment that brought us peace was upon him,
and by his wounds we are healed.

ISAIAH 53:5

SOME PEOPLE HIDE THEIR scars, but not Daddy. He showed them off.

He'd hike up his shirt and proudly show anyone who walked through the front door the scars that ran down his chest like railroad tracks. My dad had a heart problem, so when he was in his seventies, he had quadruple bypass surgery.

He knew that the surgery was necessary. To be healed he had to be wounded, and his scars were the evidence that his problem had been taken care of.

When I envision Jesus' crucifixion, my heart breaks because of the many wounds He endured for me. He was flogged, nailed to a cross, and pierced with a spear. Yet I know that His wounding was purposeful. Hundreds of years before Messiah came, the prophet Isaiah saw what it was for:

> Yet it was *our* weaknesses he carried; it was *our* sorrows that weighed him down. And we thought his troubles were a punishment from God for his own sins! But he was wounded and crushed for *our sins*. He was beaten that we might have peace. He was whipped, and we were healed!
>
> ISAIAH 53:4–5, NLT

Jesus' scars are the evidence that our sin problem has been taken care of. The purpose for His wounding, said Paul, was to take our sin and pain, to make us holy and blameless so God could adopt us as His sons and daughters, heal us, and use us.

Me? you ask. *But look at me! Look at what's happened in my life! Look at what I've done!*

The Lord knows all that, but His purpose is unwavering. So He comes in, touches all the wounded areas of our lives, and exchanges His life for our past. And it's done. Now we can move on, not looking back. We don't lose the memory of our past—that would be impossible—but we do leave it behind as done with, because that's what God has done for us.

When God looks at us now, He doesn't see our scars as reminders of our own wounded past; He sees the scars of His Son, who was wounded for us. When you begin to see yourself this way—as God sees you—you feel valued and approved. You have confidence and a sense of worth. Your past, your pain, your failures—your scars—no longer discourage.

Instead, God uses them. Redeems them. Imbues them with purpose—to fulfill the unique destiny He has designed just for you. Now instead of asking, "Lord, why did this happen to me?" you can ask, "Lord, what would You have me do with this rich history You've given me?" Instead of asking, "Lord, how can You use me after what I've done?" you can ask, "Lord, how I can help others with what I've learned from this?"

One of the great wonders of God's love is that no sin you ever commit, no pain you ever endure, is wasted. In fact, you can help others in the very areas where you yourself have wounded others and been most wounded.

You can come alongside a young man struggling with gender identity because you, too, struggled silently for many years.

You can love and empathize with the adult still suffering from the fallout of childhood abuse because you, too, lived through that nightmare.

You can help a friend recover from prescription drug dependency because you, too, had an addiction.

You can reach out to someone who has fallen into an affair because you, too, fell into sin and have lived through that devastation.

The things that have brought you the most pain and shame, the things you deplore and had hoped to dismiss, the things you thought discredit or disqualify you—these are the very things God will use to help others. As you honestly and openly share your experiences, as you admit your own failings and offer your insights, as you allow God to use your scars, you will begin to see that they are the very tools He uses to heal others. He will take the things you have done and the things that have been done to you and use them for good.

Aldous Huxley said, "Experience is not what happens to a man; it is what a man does with what happens to him."[17] Yet many of us carry around unhealed wounds that impede us. We don't allow the past to be past; we hang on to our guilt, nurse our grudges, and harbor our resentments over the painful circumstances or unjust actions of others in our lives. Like any patient, we need to heal. That may include grieving what was lost, allowing the great Surgeon to heal us, and finally coming into the wholeness God offers us through His love and grace.

When we let the Lord heal us, our wounds become scars. And when scar tissue forms, it is actually stronger than ordinary skin, stronger than the tissue it replaces. Like Christ, you no longer have wounds—you have scars, marks you carry with you for the rest of your earthly life. They are reminders that, yes, maybe you were once wounded, but now you are healed.

I sometimes envy the disciple Thomas. I don't envy him because he was skeptical and full of doubt about Jesus' resurrection, and I don't envy him the cynicism that earned him the label "doubting Thomas." I envy him because he got to touch Jesus' pierced hands and side. He got to touch the wounds that had healed him, saved him, purchased him for God.

One day, when my Redeemer welcomes me home to heaven, I will kiss His nail-scarred hands and bow in adoration at His nail-scarred feet. I will touch those wounds that saved me and brought me into His family. And I will thank Him for my own scars, which in His hands became tools He could use to bring His love and healing to others.

Lord, I never dreamed that the areas

where I have been scarred the most

are the areas where You can use me most.

Now touch and heal all the places inside me

that still feel like gaping wounds.

Turn those wounds to scars and give them purpose!

I give You my past and my experiences

—all my scars.

Redeem them and use them to

bring healing and hope to others.

Amen

22

UNFORSAKING

LOVE

God has said, "Never will I leave you;
never will I forsake you."

HEBREWS 13:5

HAVE YOU EVER BEEN
hurting so badly, struggling so much, that you thought you
would surely die? Most of us have. Or will.

Perhaps, just as I have, you've experienced times and circumstances that left you raw and bleeding—heartbreak so
severe, times so hopeless and bleak, that you were certain you
had been abandoned by all, forsaken even by God.

Jesus experienced it, too. In Gethsemane, Jesus was

sorrowful to the point of death. The unspeakable agony of Christ began that night in the garden.

Jesus knew what love would cost Him. He knew there would be mockery, torture, and bloodshed. He knew that the people He came to save would despise and reject Him, that Judas would betray Him, Peter deny Him, and His disciples abandon Him. But worst of all, He knew that His Father would forsake Him.

"Isn't there any other way?" Jesus implored in the Garden. His heart was bursting with pain. He was utterly grieved; sorrow so deep, pain so intense, heart so broken it felt like it would explode through His chest. "And being in anguish, he prayed more earnestly, and his sweat was like drops of blood falling to the ground" (Luke 22:44).

I am struck that, of the four Gospel writers, it was Luke, the physician, who described this scene—a condition that doctors today call *hematidrosis*. Jesus' intense anguish made His blood pound through His arteries, and the burst capillaries hemorrhaged into His sweat glands. His blood mixed with the sweat on the surface of His skin, making the nerve endings in the skin so sensitive that simply being *touched* magnified the intensity of the pain.[18] But Jesus was not simply touched; He was pushed, slapped, struck, bound, pierced, and whipped…experiencing physical pain at its excruciating ultimate.

Suddenly, I see the events that followed Jesus' night of anguish with new eyes. I watch in horror as the crowd presses in upon Him in the Garden. They grab Him, bind Him, and beat Him. They prod Him like an animal to the chief priests, to Pilate, then to Herod. They slap His face and strike Him with their fists. They flog Him as only Romans do, with lashes so brutal that their victims sometimes died before they could be crucified. They mash a crown of twisted thorns onto His head, then strike His head with a stick again and again, ripping His scalp wide open, ramming the sharp thorns deeper and deeper into His skull. They push a heavy, rough-hewn cross onto His back, splinters digging into His gaping wounds, and make Him walk to Golgotha carrying the instrument of His own death.

Jesus had brought His disciples to Gethsemane, as He had on many other nights. But that night He took Peter, James, and John deeper into the Garden with Him. He needed His closest companions beside Him as the darkness deepened. He didn't need them to talk to Him, counsel Him, or console Him. He just needed them to be close.

Yet Luke says, "When he rose from prayer and went back to the disciples, he found them asleep" (22:45). Just when He needed them most, they fell asleep. But Jesus didn't judge or condemn them. He knew why they fell asleep. As Luke tells us, they were "exhausted from sorrow" (v. 45). And Jesus understood. He had told them that His own soul was "over-whelmed with sorrow to the point of death" (Mark 14:34).

During the Passover meal earlier that night, Jesus had laid out the events that were about to unfold. He had broken the bread and said something strange about this being His body that would be broken for them. He had taken the cup and said it was a new covenant of His blood, poured out for many for the forgiveness of sins. He had spoken of betrayal and denial, of death and rising. It was too much for them to take in. And when they saw their friend, their Lord, stumble past them in that garden and fall with His face to the ground, crying out in grief and sorrow, with tears and sweat, it was too much. And they fell asleep, exhausted from sorrow. Jesus understood.

But know this: Even in Jesus' darkest hour, when His friends were sleeping, His Father heard His Son's cry and sent an angel to minister to Him.

But the Father knew there was one place He must abandon the Son…God forsook His Son at the cross. In all of eternity, Jesus and the Father had never been apart. They were One. But now the Son was steeped in our sin, drenched in our shame, and the Father turned away and unleashed the fury of the ages on Him. "My God, my God, why have you forsaken me?" Jesus cried out in torment (Matthew 27:46).

And then…the work was done. "It is finished!" He cried, and gave up His spirit. In that moment, the cross—the very instrument of His torture and death—became an instrument of peace, reconciling all men to the Father through the sacrifice of the Son.

Because Jesus, in His love for us, did the one thing that would cause God to forsake Him, God will never forsake one of His children. Because of what Jesus did on the cross, the Father will never give up on us. Yet sometimes in order to accomplish His purpose for our lives, He does allow us to go through our own Gethsemane. And because of His own dark hour there, Jesus understands our Gethsemane experiences. Perhaps it was that night more than any other that enabled Him to understand.

When you are struggling, desperate, in despair and turmoil, where do you turn? Family? Friends? Perhaps. But like Peter, James, and John, even your closest friends can sometimes be sleeping, unable to help you during your darkest hour. Jesus knew there was one place He could turn to find comfort, answers, and strength. "Even if my father and mother abandon me, the LORD will hold me close" (Psalm 27:10, NLT).

Love knows what it's like to be abandoned by friends; He knows what betrayal feels like. He knows what it's like to be rejected and denied, to be falsely accused, conspired against, and forsaken. He has cried and bled in a garden…and on a cross.

Love understands.

And He will never forsake you.

Lord, help me grasp the wondrous truth that

even if everyone abandons me, You never will.

You are closer than any brother.

You are nearer to me than my own breath.

When no one can really understand,

when no one else knows my pain,

when no one else stands by my side,

You stay near.

You weep with me, walk alongside me,

whisper words of comfort to me.

You will never leave me or forsake me.

Amen

23

INSPIRING

OVE

This is what God the LORD says…
who spread out the earth and all that comes out of it,
who gives breath to its people,
and life to those who walk on it:
"I, the LORD, have called you in righteousness;
I will take hold of your hand."

ISAIAH 42:5–6

LMOST ALL OF US COULD
name our "most inspiring person." For me, it's my mom.
Even though she's eighty-three, in a wheelchair, and

145

blind with macular degeneration, she's involved in countless lives and has an uplifting and ennobling effect on others. She has an indomitable spirit and a contagious optimism. That's inspiring! That's who I want to be!

My mother has stirred up my desire to be like her. In fact, that's actually what the word *inspire* means. I don't remember much from my two years of Latin in middle school, but I do recognize the Latin roots of some English words. The verb *inspirare* means "to breathe into."

That's what God does to us. Through His very breath, He gives us life and sustains us, delivers us, sends His Holy Spirit to us, and inspires us to be like Him.

The Bible says that God imparted life to the first human by breathing into him. "The LORD God formed the man from the dust of the ground and breathed into his nostrils the breath of life, and the man became a living being" (Genesis 2:7). God still breathes on us and, moment by moment, gives us life and breath. "If it were his intention and he withdrew his spirit and breath, all mankind would perish together and man would return to the dust" (Job 34:14–15).

Through the same breath that gives us life, God delivers His people. With His very breath, He parted the waters of the Red Sea and delivered the Israelites from slavery in Egypt, as they acknowledged in a song of praise: "By the blast of your nostrils the waters piled up. The surging waters stood firm like a wall; the deep waters congealed in the heart of the sea" (Exodus 15:8).

King David sang praises, too, as he witnessed God's breath of love in deliverance: "The earth trembled and quaked, the foundations of the heavens shook; they trembled because he was angry. The valleys of the sea were exposed and the foundations of the earth laid bare at the rebuke of the LORD, at the blast of breath from his nostrils" (2 Samuel 22:8, 16).

There's more. With His breath, God shows us the way to go.

He gave us the written Word: "All Scripture is God-breathed and is useful for teaching, rebuking, correcting and training in righteousness, so that the man of God may be thoroughly equipped for every good work" (2 Timothy 3:16–17).

And He gave us the Living Word—His Son. Jesus *is* the way. When Jesus died on the cross, when He breathed His last and said, "It is finished," it looked as if all was lost. But it wasn't over. Three days later God breathed life into His Son, and our resurrected King crushed Satan's head, proclaimed victory over death, and bought us freedom and life at the cost of His own.

Forty days after his crucifixion, the resurrected Christ appeared to His followers. "'Peace be with you!'" He said. "'As the Father has sent me, I am sending you.' And with that he breathed on them and said, 'Receive the Holy Spirit'" (John 20:21–22). He gave us something of Himself—something profound and sacred. Alfred, Lord Tennyson beautifully describes this gift: "Speak to Him, thou, for He hears, and Spirit with spirit can meet—Closer is He than breathing, and nearer than hands and feet."[19]

Before Jesus was crucified, He told His closest followers, "I tell you the truth: It is for your good that I am going away. Unless I go away, the Counselor will not come to you; but if I go, I will send him to you" (John 16:7). I think I finally understand why, when Jesus ascended to heaven, the Father sent us One who could not be draped in skin. His presence in our lives is deeper and more intimate than the physical, human presence Jesus ever could have been.

Only the Spirit can satisfy our yearning, our hunger to meld to God's heart and mind, as Deep calls to deep, Spirit to spirit. This love He gave us is an infusion of His very presence into ours—a saturation of His love so complete, so absorbing, that we can carry Him with us always. His life and love indwell us more deeply than blood and bone and fluid. He bypasses cells and membrane and tissue to live in the place of mystery.

Sometimes, yes, I feel His presence: a warmth, an emotional encounter, an experience. Sometimes I do not. But I don't need to. I just know. Because always the Promise is there, comforting, instructing, leading with the love of God that cannot be contained in skin. A love breathed into me by my Savior. A love closer than breath itself.

God's love inspires me to want to be like Him, and my heart cries out just as the hymn says:

> Breathe on me, Breath of God,
>   Fill me with life anew,
> That I may love what Thou dost love,
>   And do what Thou wouldst do.

Lord, my mind reels in wonder at Your majesty,

my heart pounds at Your greatness,

my lungs expand with Your Spirit.

I am overwhelmed by Your love,

which is so great it can only be expressed through three

persons—Father, Son, and Holy Spirit.

When I feel like the dry bones in Ezekiel's prophecy,

You breathe on me and renew my life.

Thank You for the inspiration of the Holy Spirit.

With every breath I join with the psalmist:

"Let everything that has breath praise the Lord!"

Amen

HEARTBREAKING

OVE

He himself bore our sins in his body on the tree,
so that we might die to sins and live for righteousness.

1 PETER 2:24

Y FRIEND BARBARA
Dodge did a painting that I love. It now hangs in my living room. It's a huge image of Jesus' head and bare chest on a canvas that is rippled and worn, yet shiny and lacquered, like His sun-baked, sweaty skin. This is a decidedly authentic-looking Jesus, dirt-smeared chest and matted hair. His eyes are clamped shut, oozing tears…and blood.

Jesus' chest is streaked red. Drops of blood from a crown

of thorns pressed into His skull drip onto flesh and run like a river down the crevice of His chest. The colors are the burnt sienna and ocher of my childhood crayon box, save for the red, the color of the blood. It's like no color I've ever seen—hues of crimson and burgundy, ruby and other-worldly jasper.

He holds a knife in His hand.

I didn't understand that at first. What did it mean? Then I saw. The knife was not for vengeance, war, or self-defense. No one had the power to kill Him. The knife is His choice—part of a plan conceived by Love, motivated out of Love, and executed by Love. Jesus chose to die. "The reason my Father loves me," He said, "is that I lay down my life—only to take it up again. No one takes it from me, but I lay it down of my own accord" (John 10:17–18).

I've always imagined that this image portrays the hours just before Jesus gave His life for ours. His eyes are closed, yet shedding bloody tears, and I feel Him speaking to me: *You wonder if I really love you? I'm doing this for you because My heart is breaking for you. I'm dying your death. I'm taking your pain. And I willingly choose to do it. This is how much I love you.*

Not too long ago, I was heartbroken over what was happening in our lives. Despite years of infertility treatment, when we finally became pregnant, we lost one baby after another to miscarriage. Two adoption attempts failed. Betrayals in relationships left us feeling heartbroken, and severe financial loss left us feeling hopeless. I was struggling with fear, resentment, and even anger at God for allowing so much loss in our lives. I so wanted to have His perspective on our circumstances, but I felt that my pleas were met with stone-cold silence. Over and over and over, I cried out, *Lord, what is Your will in all of this? Just tell me so I'll know for certain what You want me to do and how You want me to respond.*

Then I remembered that right after Jesus told His disciples that the Son of Man must suffer many things, He added: "If anyone would come after me, he must deny himself and take up his cross daily and follow me. For whoever wants to save his life will lose it, but whoever loses his life for me will save it" (Luke 9:23–24).

I sensed the Spirit's probing, sensed Him posing a disturbing and difficult question: *Will you die, too? Will you love Me as I love you? Will you willingly hand your life over to Me, as I did for you? Will you take up your cross? Will you choose the knife?*

Yes, Lord, I answered through tears. *I give You everything: my husband, my future, my life. But You have to help me. Enlarge my heart! Increase my ability to know You, to understand You, to be more like You…to love You.*

As I prayed, I saw something in my mind's eye. I saw God forcing His fingers into a jagged, narrow crevice of my heart and prying it open. It was dramatic, almost surgical— loud, cracking cartilage, bloody fluids—as He opened something that had either never been opened before, or had somehow sealed itself shut. I saw my heart and His hands. God Himself was cracking open my heart by breaking it.

One of the hard truths of the Way is this: God often achieves His purpose through heartbreaking circumstances. His purpose is always good. And it is simply this: to replace us with Himself. He allows painful, even excruciating, circumstances into our lives to crack open our hearts and replace us with Himself.

Somehow we've missed this part of the way of the Cross. We claim blessings and ministering angels, but assume that our pain is His punishment. We misconstrue His failure to help as disregard—or worse, disinterest. We're certain He has forgotten or abandoned us. We forget that He chose the knife because His heart was breaking for us.

Only when we realize that God uses *all* of our circumstances—no matter how unfair, uncomfortable, or unforeseen—to fulfill His will in our lives, can we stop struggling, questioning, and railing. Only then can we, like Him, choose the knife.

This is the great paradox of the spiritual life. It's only in dying that we have life. Dying is what we were made for. C. S. Lewis said, "He cannot bless us unless He has us. When we try to keep within us an area that is our own, we try to keep an area of death. Therefore, in love, He claims all. There's no bargaining with Him."[20]

The day God cracked open my heart was the day I finally accepted my death—death to self. When I realized that I could do nothing, that my best efforts couldn't produce a child, make me financially secure, or control others' behavior, I finally stopped struggling, rolled over, and died. I had to die to my reputation, my past, and my pride. I had to die to my fears, my doubts, and even my hopes. That day I came to the end of myself. And I have had to do that the next day, and the next, and every day since.

Every day as I gaze at that painting of Jesus in my living room, I sense Him handing me that knife in His hand, asking me to take up my cross and die to myself.

And He's asking you. *Will you die, too?*

Father, I marvel at the privilege

of living a sacrificial life of love, as You did for me.

I say yes, Lord, I choose the knife.

I give You all my expectations of what

I think my life should look like.

You laid down Your life for me;

You held nothing back.

Help me to do the same.

Once and for all, replace me with Yourself.

Amen

25

PURSUING

LOVE

Surely goodness and mercy shall follow me all the days of my life: and I will dwell in the house of the LORD for ever.

PSALM 23:6, KJV

MY STEPDAUGHTER, KATIE, was following my two-year-old grandson Blake around the house—and around and around and around.

"*Goodness!*" she exclaimed when he'd plop onto his thickly diapered bottom. She'd pick him up and off he'd scoot at breakneck speed, with Katie following hard after him. Then, boom, he'd bang into a chair or trip over those little feet and hit the floor again.

"Mercy!" she'd laugh as she picked him up yet again. (Yeah, I know. Who says "mercy" these days? But she's a Texan and Texans say things like that to their two-year-olds!) "I'm here! You're okay." She'd soothe him for a second, and off he'd go again, small legs churning, climbing onto countertops, opening cabinets. A one-toddler marathon.

I marveled at what a loving and attentive mother Katie is. She never seemed to tire of following after Blake, pursuing him wherever he went and picking him up whenever he fell. As I watched her hot on his trail, I realized that I'm just like my little grandson. I'm being followed. I'm being hounded by grace, pursued by mercy, followed by goodness and love.

And so are you.

King David knew that he was being followed, too: "Surely goodness and mercy shall follow me all the days of my life: and I will dwell in the house of the LORD for ever" (Psalm 23:6, KJV). These are God's covenant promises to His people. Different Bible versions translate this verse differently:

- "Surely your goodness and unfailing love will pursue me" (NLT).
- "Surely goodness and love will follow me" (NIV).
- "Your goodness and unfailing kindness shall be with me" (TLB).
- "Kindness and faithful love pursue me" (NJB).

It's almost as if there are not enough English words to capture the original words—these abiding promises of God, these benefits He provides to His children.

In love, He extends kindness, mercy, favor, good deeds, even loving reproach. He follows us persistently, consistently, and unconditionally. He chases us to pick us up and get us back on track. He follows us to protect us from harm. He pursues us in order to draw us near to Him and lavish us with His love.

Have you ever felt like Joseph? Betrayed and abandoned by those you trusted? His own brothers plotted against him, lied about him, and then left him for dead in a pit. But God followed Joseph into that pit. He rescued him, lifted him up, placed him in an honored position in Egypt, and ultimately used him to save the entire nation of Israel.

Have you ever felt like Elijah? Discouraged and terrified? He was a man God used to expose and destroy the prophets of Baal, but immediately after that powerful encounter, Queen Jezebel threatened to kill him, and the prophet fled in fear for his life. He had lost his confidence and concluded that his efforts were fruitless; he felt hopeless and defeated and just wanted to die. But God followed him into the desert where he'd fled, followed him under the broom tree where he'd crawled, and sent an angel to feed him bread and water and hope.

Have you ever felt like the three young Hebrews in the

book of Daniel? Penalized for doing the right thing? They were righteous young men who stood up for truth and remained faithful to the God they served. Yet they were punished for their integrity and tossed into a blazing furnace. But God followed them into the flames, and the faithfulness of the one true God shook that pagan empire to its roots.

Have you ever felt like the Samaritan woman at the well? Shamed, haunted, and desperate to be loved? She was a heartbroken woman so thirsty for love that she had given herself to others again and again, yet her thirst was never quenched. But God pursued her at that well in Samaria, satisfied her thirst with living water, and because of her, many Samaritans met Messiah.

Or maybe you've felt like Peter. He also experienced God's pursuit. As the crowds began to assemble, he adamantly denied he'd ever known Jesus, swore he'd never seen the man. Then the rooster crowed. But grace and mercy followed Peter, even into his denial. Three days later an angel gave specific instructions to the women who first arrived at Jesus' empty tomb. "Go, tell his disciples and *Peter*, 'He is going ahead of you into Galilee'" (Mark 16:7).

When the women reported this to the disciples, the men didn't believe them. It seemed like nonsense to them. But not to Peter. Luke writes: "Peter, however, got up and ran to the tomb. Bending over, he saw the strips of linen lying by themselves, and he went away, wondering to himself what had happened" (24:12). What had happened was that goodness and love had followed him right into his grief and regret. God met his denial with grace, his blunder with forgiveness and mercy.

So look around…you're being followed.

God's love seeks us out. He extends His goodness and mercy where we need it most. He follows you into your pit, your pain, your desert, your disappointment. He pursues you even in your sin and rebellion. He chases you out of your fears and straight into His arms. He is relentless in His love for you. His goodness and love will follow you despite your failures, your circumstances, and even your unbelief.

As I watch Katie run after little Blake, a loving mother tirelessly following her son with her "goodness" and "mercy," I think about our Father's pursuing love for us. And I'm struck: I always thought I was the one chasing after God. And the whole time He was running after me.

He still is.

Father, thank You for Your relentless pursuit!

Your unfailing kindness follows me into the

very places I need You most—

my fears and failures and heartaches,

even my sin and shame.

Your goodness and mercy follow me wherever I go.

In love You pursue me, to protect me, forgive me,

and draw me back into Your arms.

Amen

26

SEALING LOVE

He anointed us, set his seal of ownership on us,
and put his Spirit in our hearts as a deposit,
guaranteeing what is to come.

2 CORINTHIANS 1:21-22

URING THE CIVIL WAR, thousands of appeals for pardon came to Abraham Lincoln from soldiers sentenced to military discipline for infractions of military rules. As a rule, letters of support from influential people accompanied such appeals. The more serious the trespass, the more important it was to have letters from friends in high places.

One day an appeal came before the president from a soldier condemned to die for desertion. It was a simple request for clemency on a single sheet—without one supporting document.

"What!" Lincoln exclaimed, "Has this man no friends?"

"No, sir," said the captain, "not one."

"Then," said Lincoln, "I will be his friend."

Lincoln granted the soldier's appeal and, to make it official, sealed the paper with the presidential seal. That seal was a promise—it guaranteed the soldier a reprieve from impending judgment and death.

Just as President Lincoln used his seal to save the soldier, so God seals us from that coming day when His righteous wrath will fall upon the earth. When Jesus died on the cross, His blood permanently separated us from our sins "as far as the east is from the west" (Psalm 103:12). When we accept what He has done for us, Jesus becomes our Friend in high places—the only friend we need—and God frees us from judgment and condemnation. Then He seals us.

Sealing is the work of the Holy Spirit. In Bible times, a seal was made by rolling a small cylinder over a bit of soft clay, or by pressing a signet ring into hot wax. However it was done, the material had to be pliable enough to receive the impression. The same is true of us. If our hearts are hard, God has to soften us before He can seal us. So He sends the Holy Spirit to woo us to Christ, softening our hearts until we are able to respond to His love and yield to Him. And when we do, this same Spirit seals us. "Having believed, you were marked in him with a seal, the promised Holy Spirit, who is a deposit guaranteeing our inheritance" (Ephesians 1:13–14).

Have you ever asked yourself what this inheritance means? I think most of us tend to think of the obvious. When we die, we'll go to heaven and see the Lord face-to-face. That alone is overwhelming. But God has an inheritance for you right here and right now. His seal guarantees that your life will have purpose and meaning long before you settle into your mansion in the sky.

Now you may be looking at your life and wondering, *How could God have plans for a person with my history?* I'm sure Zerubbabel must have felt the same way. Although he was a direct descendant of King David, Zerubbabel was also the grandson of King Jehoiachin, a man so wicked that God said to him, "Even if you...were a signet ring on my right hand, I would still pull you off" (Jeremiah 22:24). The prophet Jeremiah prophesied that none of Jehoiachin's descendants would ever prosper or "sit on the throne of David" (22:30).

Then along came Zerubbabel, who loved God and obeyed Him. And what did God do? He instructed the prophet Haggai to tell Zerubbabel that He had great plans for him. "'I will make you like my signet ring, for I have chosen you,' declares the LORD Almighty" (Haggai 2:23). In essence, Zerubbabel's faith broke the family curse...and changed the course of history. Christ, who was directly descended from him, will sit on the throne of David forever.

It doesn't matter what you have done or what has been done to you. God has a plan for you, and He sends his Holy Spirit to reveal it to You.

That's not all.

This God, who loved you so much that He didn't spare even His own Son, who has a purpose and a plan for your life, also freely gives you *all things.* Can you fathom all God has in mind for you? Can you get even an inkling of all the marvelous gifts He pours out to you every moment of every day? Paul says it's impossible to grasp: "No eye has seen, no ear has heard, no mind has conceived what God has prepared for those who love him" (1 Corinthians 2:9).

But wait.

Read the next verse: "But *you've* seen and heard it because God by his Spirit has brought it all out into the open before you" (v. 10, *The Message*). This benevolent King, this generous Father, this lavishing God so wants us to grasp the enormity of His love that He pours out even more of Himself through the Holy Spirit, who whispers His love thoughts and reveals the secrets of His counsel. The NLT says it this way:

> But we know these things because God has revealed them to us by his Spirit, and his Spirit searches out everything and shows us even God's deep secrets. No one can know what anyone else is really think-

ing except that person alone, and no one can know God's thoughts except God's own Spirit. And God has actually given us his Spirit (not the world's spirit) so we can know the wonderful things God has freely given us.

vv. 10–12

When Larry and I were married, I gave him a wedding band with a Scripture engraved inside: "Place me like a seal over your heart" (Song of Solomon 8:6). It is an etched guarantee of my love, a seal of my covenant promise. That's what the Holy Spirit is to us. When we believe in His Son, God seals us for all eternity, guaranteeing what is to come. "And hope does not disappoint us, because God has poured out his love into our hearts by the Holy Spirit, whom he has given us" (Romans 5:5).

That's a guarantee—signed, sealed, delivered!

Lord, thank You that Your life is

indelibly stamped into me because of Jesus

and I am sealed as Yours by the Holy Spirit,

Your covenant promise of Your great love for me.

Continue to reveal more and more of

Your heart, Your ways, and Your truth to me.

Continue to pour out the love of

the Father into my heart.

Fill me to overflowing, anoint me,

and lead me, precious Holy Spirit.

Amen

RESPONSIVE

OVE

"Which of you, if his son asks for bread, will give him a stone?
If you, then, though you are evil,
know how to give good gifts to your children,
how much more will your Father in
heaven give good gifts to those who ask him!"

MATTHEW 7:9, 11

*W*HAT DO YOU WANT ME
to do for you?"

Jesus asked that question time and again.

"What do you want Me to do for you?" He asked the
blind beggar.

It seems the answer would have been self-evident. This was a *blind* man, groping his way along to stand before Jesus. His need was so apparent, so obvious. Even so, Jesus asked and waited for the answer.

"Rabbi," said the blind man, "I want to see."

Jesus gave this man just what he asked for. He met him at his point of need and gave the man his sight. But the Lord doesn't always do that. He doesn't always give us just what we ask for. Sometimes when we ask for one thing, He gives us something else.

"What do you want Me to do for you?" Jesus asked James and John, His closest disciples.

"Let one of us sit at your right and the other at your left in your glory," they replied (Mark 10:37). This was like asking Jesus to make them CEO and CFO of His new kingdom.

What I find amazing is the timing of their petition. Mark tells us that they made their request immediately after Jesus predicted His death, explained what would be happening to Him, and told His disciples what they should expect. He was about to be betrayed, mocked, flogged, spit on, condemned to death, and crucified.

The Lord had just spelled out His coming death, detail by heartbreaking detail. And then He told them the greatest news and most wondrous miracle of all—that He would be raised again to life. And on the heels of *that,* here come these two (in fact, three—Matthew's account of the story says their ambitious stage mother was in on it, too), angling for position, negotiating for rank in the kingdom they still believed Jesus was about to set up.

Unbelievable.

"You don't know what you are asking," Jesus told them politely (v. 38).

When Jesus asks us, "What do you want Me to do for you?" and we tell Him, do we always know what we're asking? We can't see the big picture or even begin to comprehend what is really best for us. That's why Jesus, in His wise and protective love, sometimes answers our heartfelt requests with "no" or "not now." That's why He asks us to simply place our trust in Him, believe He has our best interests at heart, and wait for Him to work in our lives according to His will.

Then again, maybe we're too afraid or discouraged or beaten down to ask at all. Perhaps we suffer from what Robert Louis Stevenson called the "malady of not wanting."[21] Jesus knew about that, too. At the pool of Bethesda, He saw a man lying among the disabled. When He learned he'd been an invalid for thirty-eight years, Jesus asked him, "Do you want to get well?" (John 5:6).

Some of us have lost the will to ask to be whole. We're disappointed and hopeless, disillusioned and weary. Or perhaps we've grown comfortable in our "condition," a victim, responding with "yeah, but's" and "if only's," complacently sitting by, waiting for the pool to be stirred or for someone else to help us into the water. Day after day, month after month, year after year.

"Do you want to get well?" Jesus asks. "What do you want?"

He once said that we don't have because we don't ask. In love, God responds to our requests and gives us what we truly need. To the blind beggar He gave sight so he could see what Love looks like. To the cripple He gave a new beginning. To James He gave the grace to drink the same cup and be baptized with the same baptism He Himself endured—a martyr's death. To John He gave spiritual eyesight and the grace to deeply love.

How long has it been since you've opened up your heart in God's presence and told Him exactly what you want? (He already knows, but He still wants you to ask.) What's on your secret list? Do you want Him to do something *for* you...or something *in* you? Do you want achievement and possessions...or character? Do you want to have and to do...or to be? What do you really want from Him? I have a feeling that God's favorite response to His Son's question, the petition He will move all of earth and heaven itself to grant, is this: "I want to love as You love. I want to be like You."

One day, John the Baptist's disciples saw Jesus, and when they realized He could be the One they'd been waiting for, they immediately followed Him. Jesus saw them, turned, and asked, "What do you want?" (John 1:38).

My heart leaps, as theirs must have, and my answer is the

same: "I want to know where You're staying…. I want to know who You are…. I want to be near You…. I want…want…"

His wild yet tender otherworldly eyes bore into mine. "Come," He says, "and you will see" (v. 39). Just that. The invitation is both intimate and universal, for me alone and for all mankind. I want to follow Love, just as they did.

In His love, God is committed to making us like His Son. That's the greatest ambition we could ever have and the most important request we could ever make. And it is what God most wants to give us. If only we would ask…and then follow Him.

What do you want God to do for you?

Lord, I invite you to examine the depths of my heart.

When you ask me the question, "What do you want?"

I confess that I don't always know the answer....

Sometimes I don't desire enough,

so ignite my faith, restore lost hope.

Sometimes I desire amiss, so root out pride,

greed, and selfish ambition.

Give me the desires of Your heart so that when

You ask, "What do you want?"

my answer will be pleasing to You.

My heartfelt desire will be to follow You,

my deepest longing, to love like You and become like You.

Amen

LAVISHING

LOVE

How great is the love the Father has lavished on us,
that we should be called children of God!
And that is what we are!

1 JOHN 3:1

MY GRANDDADDY WAS A shipbuilder, strong as an ox, hard as a rock. His huge, burly chest and back were tanned like shoe leather and just as rough. He had a booming voice you could hear clear down the block. He didn't talk, really. He bellowed. He was pretty scary.

Every Sunday afternoon my parents, my brother, Tracy,

and I would drive from Ft. Lauderdale to Miami to visit Granddaddy. We'd sit out on his big front porch in the white Adirondack chairs he'd built, drink sweet tea from mason jars, and listen to his stories. When I was little, I'd sidle up next to him, and he'd yank me up onto his lap. His hands were rough, he smelled of tobacco, and his voice was so loud that soon I'd slide down and retreat to the comfort of my mom's lap.

Granddaddy used to go wild boar hunting in the Everglades with my Uncle David. They'd load up Granddaddy's truck with rope and his pit bull, Ring. Granddaddy liked to hunt the old-fashioned way. Ring would get on a scent, run after the hog, grab it by its ear, and start baying. Then Granddaddy and Uncle David would run like thunder toward him through palmettos and grasslands, dodging saw grass and sinkholes and gators.

Granddaddy always got there first. He'd take the rope off his belt and wrap it round and round the flailing hog's sharp hooves, and then he and Uncle David would carry the boar miles back to the truck. When he turned thirty-five, Uncle David couldn't keep up with Granddaddy anymore, and he called it quits. So Granddaddy hunted by himself. He wasn't just scary—he was tough!

But he was also a softie. He had a tender and generous heart beneath that gruff exterior. Through the years his old neighborhood in Miami had become home to more and more Cuban immigrants, and the Cuban kids loved

Granddaddy. They seemed to see right through that rough veneer. Giggling, they'd dive into his lap and climb all over him.

And Granddaddy loved those kids as much as they loved him. He would drive all over Miami looking in trash heaps for broken bikes and toys and wagons. He'd bring them home, fix them up, and set them out in front of his house near the street. Soon a couple of kids would come to his door and shout, "Sawyer!" (They always called him by his last name.) When my granddad would come to the door, they'd ask in broken English, "Sawyer, can we play with this?"

"*No!*" he'd bellow…and slam the screen door behind him. Then he'd turn around, step back outside, and softly— albeit gruffly—say, "But you can *have* it." They would squeal in delight, stretch their arms wide to hug him tight around the waist, and dash back into the yard, shouting, "Gracias, Sawyer!" over their shoulders.

Those kids taught me a lot about my granddad. I thought he should be gentle, affectionate, and approachable. After all, that's what a grandfather is supposed to be, right? But those kids saw who my granddad really was. They saw right through the brusqueness and into his heart. They knew him. They grasped his character and his nature. They didn't speak much English, but they recognized the language that he spoke best. My granddad was lavishing them with love.

Somehow, he reminds me of another Father—One who

lavishes His children with love beyond imagination or description.

> How great is the love the Father has lavished on us,
> that we should be called children of God! And that
> is what we are! The reason the world does not know
> us is that it did not know him.
>
> 1 JOHN 3:1

I tend to forget about that last sentence. Don't you? The world doesn't know God as He really is. Sometimes, neither do we. And because we don't know Him well enough, we don't always realize that He's lavishing love upon us.

The way I perceived my granddad when I was a child is so often the way we perceive God. We see Him as hard, scary, or unapproachable. We think of thunder, celestial frowns, and a distant throne among the stars. He's not the soft, cuddly God we might have been looking for. But no matter what our impressions, God is always lavishing love on us, just as Granddaddy lavished it on those children.

God always has us in mind. He looks for ways to bless us and for treasures to bestow on us. He loves to take the broken things in our lives and make them like new. He repairs our battered hearts, restores our damaged pasts, and re-creates our shattered dreams. And He loves it when, unhindered and unafraid, we run into His presence, throw our arms around Him, and help ourselves to His love. He showers us with joys and pleasures, fills us with life and hope, and gives us a part of Himself.

Our part is simply to see God as He is, to get past our preconceived ideas of who He is (or isn't), and to become acquainted with Him. He wants us to have more than a superficial knowledge of Him based on soft, fuzzy feelings or worn-out Sunday-school clichés. What's more, He wants us to have a *true* picture of Him, not one skewed by past hurts or false perceptions. He wants us to know His character, His heart, and His ways. And the more we get to know the God of the Scriptures, the more we begin to understand Him and glimpse the truth of who He is, the more we'll see all the ways He's lavishing His love on us.

Lord, I realize that I don't always
see You as You really are.
Forgive me for any false perceptions I have of You.
Open my eyes and my heart so
I can know You better.
Help me to see all the ways You are
showering me with Your love,
even when I don't realize it.
Make me more like a little child,
uninhibited and unafraid,
racing with abandon into Your arms,
and receiving with delight all
the love You lavish on me.
Amen

UNHURRIED

OVE

Be still before the LORD
and wait patiently for him.

PSALM 37:7

I HAVE THIS RECURRING
nightmare. I'm standing in front of a roomful of people who
look a lot like me.

"Hi, I'm Nancy," I say, "and I have a confession."

"Hi, Nancy!" they bellow in unison.

"I'm an addict," I say.

Then I wake up.

In my dream I never get to finish making my confession.

But right now—in cold type—I finally will. I never dreamed I'd make it in this kind of public forum, but here goes….

My name is Nancy, and I have a serious addiction. I'm addicted to adrenaline.

There, I've said it. I feel freer already. Confession *is* good for the soul.

Now give me another fix. Go ahead—hit me with a blissful shot of fast pace, rushing, breakneck speed, jam-packed schedule, and busyness. Aaah…thanks…better now…no more white space in that Day-Timer, got my PDA and DSL; got my laptop fired up, a fax coming in, and my cell phone's ringing…good, good, good…. Yeah, here it comes—that good ol' familiar feeling. O-kay…. Well, I'm off again. See you at the next meeting.

Busyness is what makes me feel the best. My body *likes* the feeling adrenaline releases into my brain. It's gotten used to my cortisol levels shooting through the roof, my heart racing out of my chest, my synapses firing. It's an actual physical dependence. But it's also an emotional one. Truth be told, rushing, racing, feeling hurried, harried, and harassed makes me feel—important.

The trouble is, the busier and more "productive" I am, the more impatient and judgmental I become of others who don't have the same compulsive pace. Never mind that they may actually be accomplishing more or doing more meaningful work. Never mind that their activities may be more in tune with the Holy Spirit, that they're listening for His voice and leading. Never mind…they're just so *slow*.

I complain and mutter and moan about the hectic pace of life, but don't really do anything to change it. I wouldn't dare! Because if this speeding car came to a grinding halt, what then? I'd be forced to stop and look at my life, look at what I'm running from, what I'm running toward, what's driving this engine, and what it was that got me behind the wheel in the first place.

That's what's really behind most addictions. They keep us from looking at what's going on inside us. My progressively increasing speed successfully diverts me from the uncertainty—and sheer terror—of confronting myself.

If I slow down, get off the treadmill, give up the adrenaline rush—what will my life be like? If I'm not making things happen, being productive, doing something, will I be accepted? Feel valued and liked? Will I like myself? And perhaps most scary of all, will God like and accept me? The uncertainty is terrifying—so I keep my pedal to the metal and just keep driving. I drive till my wheels fall off, complaining as I go and missing out on what's really important.

Jesus' friend Martha was like that.

When Jesus came for a visit, Martha's sister, Mary, sat enraptured at His feet, listening to all He said. Martha, however, ran around "distracted by all the preparations that had to be made," writes Luke. When she complained, Jesus chided her with a gentle rebuke. "'Martha, Martha,' the Lord answered, 'you are worried and upset about many things, but only one thing is needed. Mary has chosen what is better, and it will not be taken away from her'" (10:40–42).

Now fast-forward to another dinner. In John 12:1–3, Mary is still at Jesus' feet, and Martha is still serving. But Martha isn't harassed and complaining—even though she's serving seventeen guests this time instead of four. Something has changed.

Martha has finally learned to "be still, and know that I am God" (Psalm 46:10), and she feels the sweet, inexplicable peace that flows from that decision.

As her sister, Mary, pours out the pint of nard and wipes Jesus' feet with her hair, as the house fills with the fragrance of that perfume, Martha's heart fills with love for her Lord. She's discovered the "one thing needed"; she's "chosen what is better." And as she serves Him and His friends from this new attitude of worship, her meal and hospitality are every bit as fragrant an offering of devotion to Jesus as Mary's.

Martha was becoming more like her Savior. Jesus was never in a hurry. He took time to go apart and listen to the Father. He welcomed interruptions as opportunities to minister, yet accomplished all the work God gave Him to do. And He took time to slip away with His friends to rest and relax. "The apostles returned to Jesus from their ministry tour and told him all they had done.... Then Jesus said, 'Let's get away from the crowds for a while and rest'" (Mark 6:30–31, NLT).

Like Martha, I'm learning to live this better way...and

loving it. The old ways of living, the old ways of thinking and being, no longer satisfy. A slower pace keeps us in rhythm with God's heart and leading, helping us listen, learn, and grow deeper every day.

There's a journey to be made here, a sojourn to take. If we have the courage and patience to be still, it will lead us directly to the heart of our Lover. There He soothes us with the precious balm of Gilead, heals our fractured hearts and wounded spirits, and draws us into secret chambers of intimacy with Him.

It's here, in this place of unhurried communion, that you get to know Him, that you experience His love. You peel open your soul, let Him into those dusty places you'd cordoned off, and allow the deepest and most tender intimacies flow between you…Deep calling unto deep.

And as I settle down here at Your feet, dear Lord, and break open my own vial of love and adoration and worship, I feel it—my heart racing, pounding in my chest. This time, not from adrenaline—but from love for You.

And I'm becoming addicted to this feeling.

Dearest Friend and Savior,

I love this unhurried, unbridled time with You.

I love this journey into the depths of Your heart.

I fall headlong at Your feet, and into Your arms.

I quiet my heart and listen to Yours.

I feel Your love and pour out mine.

Help me live in this place of deep intimacy

with You every single day of my life.

Amen

NOURISHING

LOVE

Taste and see that the LORD is good.

PSALM 34:8

AFTER A RECENT SPEAKING engagement in South Dakota, my lovely host, Dorcas, shuttled me across seventy miles of beautiful farm country to the bustling airport at Pierre (properly pronounced *pier*, thank you very much).

I wanted to be sure I made my plane back to Los Angeles, and since we were running a skosh late, we pulled into a fast-food restaurant so we could eat on the run. As soon as we placed our order, we heard a young man's voice over the speaker.

"Your order will be ready in 224 seconds. Is that all right?"

Dorcas and I looked at each other and giggled.

"Excuse me?" I asked the intercom.

"Your order will be ready in…203 seconds. Can you wait?"

We were so tickled we couldn't help ourselves, "I'm sorry, what did you say?"

"Your order will be ready in 172 seconds."

We waited a bit, and then Dorcas asked, "How many now?"

"Uh…47."

Then, an unsolicited update: "Just 19 more seconds to go."

Pretty soon, the voice popped its sixteen-year-old head through the window with a bag of piping hot hamburgers and perfectly fried fries. "Wow," he said. "I'm really sorry it took so long. Thank you *so* much for being patient."

Boy! I thought. *We've really taken instant gratification to new heights! This poor kid was worried we'd be irritated if it took 224 seconds to get our food.*

As I thought about this on the plane ride home, it occurred to me that this demand for instant nourishment has made its way into our spiritual lives as well. Instead of making the world like the kingdom, we've made the kingdom just like the world. We've reduced the kingdom of God to the Burger Kingdom.

We work fast and furious, running our lives our way in our own strength until we're famished, and then think, *Maybe I need a little spiritual nourishment.* So we whip in, bark our order into the speaker, wait a few seconds, and then hit the road again, without ever having to leave the comfort of our air-conditioned sedan. We merge back into the fast lane, gobble our manna on the run, and grumble that it took more than 224 seconds to get it.

Hmmm. Manna…grumble. Sounds familiar. It's not the first time those words have been linked. In another time and another place, another group of people complained about the daily ration of fast food. Even so, God rained down nourishment like clockwork, dishing down regular provision for all their needs.

But all along God had a more perfect sustenance in mind. Manna was just a foretaste of an infinitely better kind of bread. Manna was temporary; this Bread is eternal:

> "I am the bread of life. He who comes to me will never go hungry, and he who believes in me will never be thirsty. Whoever eats my flesh and drinks my blood has eternal life, and I will raise him up at the last day…. Your forefathers ate manna and died, but he who feeds on this bread will live forever."
>
> JOHN 6:35, 54, 58

Manna was gathered on the run and eaten quickly before it spoiled; this Bread lasts forever and only improves the longer it is savored. Manna might have been tasty, but it became monotonous. The Bread of Life has a flavor that continually delights, endlessly satisfies. Manna provided bare-bones nutrition to sustain life; this Bread provides nourishment that gives life to the full.

Just as He did at a wedding in Cana, turning well water into fine wine, Jesus transforms the ordinary into the extraordinary. Just as He did for the five thousand on a hillside, He multiplies paltry portions into abundance. And just as He offered His own body as the sacrifice for all, He still gives the "food that endures to eternal life…the bread of God is he who comes down from heaven and gives life to the world" (John 6:27, 33).

He invites us to "taste and see that the LORD is good" (Psalm 34:8). As in the tradition of the age, He invites us to recline on the couch, linger at His banqueting table spread lush with delights, and savor its bounty. "The king was at his table…. I delight to sit in his shade, and his fruit is sweet to my taste. He has taken me to the banquet hall, and his banner over me is love" (Song of Solomon 1:12; 2:3–4). And the longer we linger there, the more satisfied we become. The more slowly we eat this Bread, the more health we enjoy. The more we digest this Word-made-flesh, the more life we possess. The more we savor His presence, the more like Him we become.

This Bread of Life tastes divine and satisfies completely.

And yet there is a greater feast that still awaits. A handwritten invitation, sealed by the King, invites us to the ultimate banquet, where sounds of a great multitude and the roar of rushing waters and loud peals of thunder shout, "Hallelujah! For our Lord God Almighty reigns. Let us rejoice and be glad and give him glory! For the wedding of the Lamb has come, and his bride has made herself ready…. 'Blessed are those who are invited to the wedding supper of the Lamb!'" (Revelation 19:6–7, 9).

If you know Jesus Christ as Savior, you *are* invited. Somewhere in the unimaginable splendor of the Other Side, there is a place setting with your name on it. But you needn't save up your appetite for *then*. The feasting begins now. The fresh, fragrant Bread of Life is always within reach…and it will never, ever disappoint.

Lord, forgive me for taking

our relationship for granted,

for rushing through our time together.

I know that You desire for me to

leisurely recline at Your table,

to taste and see that You are good.

I accept Your invitation.

Help me to linger with You, savor Your sweet love,

come to know You more deeply and intimately.

And as I do, Your life in me brings

growth and healing, life and joy.

Amen

IMMEASURABLE

OVE

I pray that you, being rooted and established in love,
may grasp how wide and long and
high and deep is the love of Christ.

WAS TRYING TO HELP MY
godson with his geometry.

Noble idea, but I soon found myself completely out of
my element, and my eyes began to glaze over. Give me
Dickens or Emerson or Austen and I'm there, but the
Pythagorean theorem is Greek to me. I can't even *find* the
hypotenuse, much less measure it. But there we were, meas-

uring lines and angles and shapes. Algorithms, parallelo-grams, spatial modeling… My head was reeling.

And then, seemingly out of nowhere, something amaz-ing emerged on the page. A horizontal line stretching from margin to margin intersected with a vertical line running the length of the page.

A cross. I smiled.

Malcolm Muggeridge once said, "The material universe is…a message in code from God."[22] And there on the graph paper was a picture of God's immeasurable love—in code. All I could think about was Paul's prayer that we would somehow grasp the extent of God's measureless love:

> I pray that out of his glorious riches he may strengthen you with power through his Spirit in your inner being, so that Christ may dwell in your hearts through faith. And I pray that you, being rooted and established in love, may have power, together with all the saints, to grasp how wide and long and high and deep is the love of Christ, and to know this love that surpasses knowledge—that you may be filled to the measure of all the fullness of God.
>
> EPHESIANS 3:16–19

Extravagant dimensions. No matter how we try to calcu-late it in our finite little brains, no matter how much math we know or how much computer wizardry we use, we can't even come close to measuring how wide and long and high and deep is the love of Christ. The magnitude of His love is, quite simply, immeasurable.

God went to all lengths to redeem you. He stretched through time and space to reach out to you and sent His own Son to free you. From the most exalted position in the universe, from its outermost, uppermost limits, He bent down to touch you and call you by name. On the cross, He spread His arms wide to embrace you, accept you, and include you.

God's love spans the width of the universe and the length of eternity; it reaches from the heights of heaven to the depths of hell. "From everlasting to everlasting," David wrote, "the LORD's love is with those who fear him" (Psalm 103:17). And again, "Where can I go from your Spirit? Where can I flee from your presence? If I go up to the heavens, you are there; if I make my bed in the depths, you are there" (139:7–8).

His love stretches across the gaping chasm our sin has created between us. It reaches deep into the darkest recesses of our self-loathing and destruction. It soars beyond our doubts and fears, soothes our trembling hearts, and strengthens our weak knees. His love bends low to meet us and lifts our chin to gaze into His eyes.

God's love is pursuing, proactive, and persevering. "God demonstrates his own love for us in this: While we were still sinners, Christ died for us" (Romans 5:8).

He loves us when we are mired neck-deep in the waste of our own making.

He loves us when we are destitute and have nothing to offer Him.

He loves us when we turn our backs on Him and walk away.

He loves us when we run in the opposite direction.

He loves us when we destroy our lives—and even the lives of others.

He loves us when we stumble and fall, and fall yet again.

He loves us when we curse Him, deny Him, defy Him.

He loves us. He can do nothing less. He is God, and God is love.

As my godson measured the intersecting lines, I looked over his shoulder and marveled at the perfect cross. Why would a holy God care so deeply for *me*? Unholy, unworthy, unimportant me? King David marveled at it, too: "When I consider your heavens, the work of your fingers, the moon and the stars, which you have set in place, what is man that you are mindful of him, the son of man that you care for him?" (Psalm 8:3–4).

Though I don't understand why God loves us so immeasurably, I know that He does and that He reveals His love in everything He has created. "From the intrinsic evidence of His creation," wrote Sir James Hopwood Jeans, "the Great Architect of the universe now begins to appear as a pure mathematician."[23]

Now, in time and space, we can only grasp what's on the page. But the lines do not end at the margins of the page; they continue to infinity. Paul's prayer for us will perhaps only be fully realized in eternity. Meanwhile, with wide-eyed wonder, I gaze at God's mathematical code: two intersecting lines of a cross—the irrefutable, eternal, and exact truth of His immeasurable love.

Father, thank You for Your measureless love.

Thank You that You would send

Your own Son to die on a cross for me.

When I am tempted to believe that You have

forgotten or abandoned me,

when I fear that my failings will drive You away,

remind me of those intersecting lines on the page.

There is nowhere I can go,

nothing I can do that can separate me from You.

Help me to fully experience the

length, depth, width, and breadth

of Your immeasurable love for me!

Amen

A LIFE OF WONDER

Show the wonder of your great love.

PSALM 17:7

IN THE TIME WE'VE SPENT together, we've barely waded our toe into the vastness of God's love. This is just the beginning of the journey God has planned for you, the untold wonders He wants to reveal to you. So don't hold back. Venture farther out into the depths with Him, and dive into His waiting arms. Live a life of wonder! One day I hope to meet you face-to-face, to hear about your journey into the heart of God and your stories of the wonders of His love.

Your friend,

Nancy

Also, you can visit me at my website:
www.nancystafford.com

PAGES FOR REFLECTION

Notes

1. Charles Williams, *Taliessin Through Logres, The Region of the Summer Stars, Arthurian Torso* (Grand Rapids, MI: Eerdmans, 1974), 291.

2. C. S. Lewis, *Mere Christianity* (New York: Macmillan, 1954), 179.

3. Stefan Zweig, "Let Us Rejoice at Our Trials," from *Jeremias*.

4. Oswald Chambers, *My Utmost for His Highest* (New York: Dodd Mead and Company, 1935).

5. Max Lucado, *The Glory of Christmas* (Dallas, TX: Word Publishing, 1996), 80.

6. Henry Wadsworth Longfellow, from "The Children of the Lord's Supper."

7. C. S. Lewis, *God in the Dock: Essays on Theology and Ethics* (Grand Rapids, MI: Eerdmans, 1970), 148.

8. C. S. Lewis, *The Four Loves* (New York: Harcourt Brace Jovanovich, 1960), 38.

9. Maimonides, quoted in *The Oxford Dictionary of Quotations* (Oxford: Oxford University Press, 1999), 491.

10. Charles Spurgeon, *Morning and Evening,* Morning October 22. http://www.morningandevening.org/ME1022XM.htm (accessed 19 February 2004).

11. Ibid., Morning December 20.

12. Cited in Tryon Edwards, D.D., *Useful Quotations Prose and Poetical* (New York: Grosset & Dunlap, 1933), 354.

13. Chambers, *My Utmost for His Highest*, 166.

14. Ibid., 167.

15. Victoria Clayton, "Psychology by the Square Foot," *Los Angeles Times,* 10 August 2003, 12.

16. Ibid.

17. Aldous Huxley, "Texts and Pretexts, Introduction (1932)," in Robert Andrews, Mary Biggs, and Michael Seidel, *The Columbia World of Quotations* (New York: Columbia University Press, 1996), number 29961.

18. Erven Park, "An Agony Unbeknown," *Seattle Catholic*, 23 March 2002; 21 Aug 2003, http://www.seattlecatholic.com/article_20020323_An_Agony_ Unbeknown.html (accessed 17 February 2004).

19. Alfred, Lord Tennyson, "The Higher Pantheism" as quoted in Leonard Roy Frank, *Random House Webster's Quotationary* (New York: Random House Reference, 2001), 317.

20. C. S. Lewis, "A Slip of the Tongue," *The Weight of Glory and Other Addresses* (New York: Macmillan, 1980), 130.

21. Robert Louis Stevenson, *The Master of Ballantrae.*

22. Malcolm Muggeridge, *Jesus Rediscovered,* 1.1, 1969, as quoted in Frank, *Random House Webster's Quotationary*, 322.

23. Sir James Hopwood Jeans, *The Mysterious Universe,* 5, 1930, as quoted in Frank, *Random House Webster's Quotationary*, 495.

"Honest, transparent, and liberating."
—MICHELLE MCKINNEY HAMMOND

In an intimate dialogue, Nancy Stafford bares her heart to readers, giving her own refreshing answer to our culture's judgments about appearance. She reflects on *true* beauty— the beauty women discover through God's acceptance, where they find "freedom from our pasts and freedom from the bondage of our image-obsessed culture."

Turn away from the mirror that condemns you, and face the transforming love of Jesus Christ.

1-57673-950-3

"Nancy builds a bridge to connect the inside and the outside. The result is the revelation of a beauty that will heal."
—HENRY CLOUD, PHD

Available at Christian bookstores everywhere

www.multnomahbooks.com

Your Personal Study Guide to Finding Identity,
Value, and True Beauty

BEAUTY BY THE BOOK STUDY GUIDE

Visit www.nancystafford.com for a free download

1-57673-950-3

Nancy has developed this free
downloadable study guide for:

∽ *personal devotions*

∽ *small groups*

∽ *women's ministries*

∽ *college or high school girls*

Use this study to dig deeper and spend some time in
honest reflection with God.

For more information about Nancy Stafford,
or to book Nancy to speak at your event or retreat, please visit:
www.nancystafford.com
or e-mail
ns@nancystafford.com
PO Box 11807, Marina del Rey, CA 90295

Printed in the United States
by Baker & Taylor Publisher Services